Through and Beyond TOGETHER

How to find victory over adversity with "The Wonderful Counsellor"

By David H. Walker

PRESS

To Paddy Barrett as a symbol of the debt of gratitude which I owe to you for some really important learning experiences afforded during my formative years in Probation in Hampshire (pages 44 – 88 inclusive)

With the wisdom of hindsight, I know that God was guiding me into just the right paths and you and Adrian Stanley were really helpful in ways one only realises later.

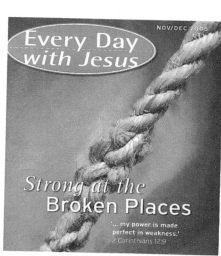

NOV/DEC 2005

Every Day with Jesus

Strong at the Broken Places

'... my power is made perfect in weakness.'
2 Corinthians 12:9

So this book is one small way of saying a big THANK YOU –

and may God continue to richly bless you

Agape.

David W

Thank you CWR
for allowing us to share the
truths which dear
Selwyn Hughes
led us into just before he
was promoted to Glory.

David H Walker   March 2012

David H. Walker
9 The Manor, Churchdown
Gloucester   GL3 2HT

Acknowledgements

E ven though I was not always aware of its importance, I acknowledge the continuing influence over my life by the "Lord of Sea and Sky"[21] who seemed to wake me at 4am at crucial points in my life. My story revolves around the loving care from my family in England and in USA, during and after the Second World War, which is why I am pleased that Xulon Press is publishing on both sides of the Atlantic. I thank my wife Mary for her patience and sacrificial love over 52 Golden years. Without the miraculous healing of our Saviour, nothing which this book celebrates would have been possible.

I am so grateful that, former Chief Executive of the UK Association of Christian Counsellors (ACC), David Depledge, has contributed a Foreword.. My mentor, Revd David Bick, has just had his book, "Let your faith grow" published. I am grateful to his publishers, O Books for allowing the cover which show the peaceful view of Gloucester Cathedral from St Josephs, the home of David Bick. During more than 20 years my faith grew, guided by his wisdom. The autobiographical sections of this book have been inspired by my emerging belief that the first thirty years of my life prepared the way for me to be one of many pioneers in a wonderful new profession in "Christian Counselling". People who wanted to change their lifestyle found new peace through confidential, focussed conversation with trained counsellors who brought the offer of a prayerful emphasis.

I acknowledge the great help I received in preparation of this new service from many former colleagues and close friends.

Their shared fellowship and fun as we entered new territory enriched our journeys together. My artist and photographer friend Graham Abbott has enabled telling this story book to be more colourful. There have been numerous helpful criticisms from Greta Randle (CEO of ACC), Sheila Jacob (professional author), and not least from my sister Dr.Averil Stedeford. Their contributions enabled me to tell the story better, and I thank them for frank comments which often caused be to rewrite large sections. I thank the publishers of "Everyday with Jesus for allowing me to use the cover of one edition of the notes of Rev Selwyn Hughes. These have guided my daily devotions for 30 years, and enriched my love and understanding of scripture.

So many people have been influential in my life, which is why the word "TOGETHER" is so important. Rev Vernon Godden and his wife Maureen were there at many crucial points, but so were David Watkins a leader of an evangelical church. The whole spectrum of churchmanship was included in our teams, and I revelled in learning from our differences. We were ploughing new furrows together – guided by the Good Shepherd. I am especially grateful to nine people who came for help when on the edge of despair, who have told their stories so graphically – with the benefit of hindsight. May their brave witness inspire you.

It is an adventure writing a book for the first time. I have often felt like abandoning it, but there have been many encouragers. I know that many others in ACC could tell similar stories better, but I do pray that you will enjoy this true story of how God does carry us around all the bumps and usually into peaceful and more creative times.

"With Him, all things are possible" To him be the glory!

Foreword
by David Depledge

Former Chief Executive UK Association of Christian Counsellors There are about 7 billion of us living on this planet, and each one has a unique story. So is one man's story worth telling? Is it a story of everything going wonderfully well and earth shattering achievements? Well, no. Not everything did go well for David Walker, but overcoming difficulties and setbacks, disappointments and losses is one way in which we can learn and develop in our time on earth. Certainly David has had some significant achievements, as you will read, but they are not on a world scale. Like millions of others, he has made a difference to the relatively few people that have come into his orbit, in the relatively small area of the world in which he has lived and worked.

But I want to say that individual testimony is powerful indeed. When you meet David Walker you will find that he is a gentle and humble man. But he is one who has worked to bring restoration to murderers and rapists. He has also faced the sadness of dealing with those who were not looking for restoration. Testimony can be our inspiration to do something worthwhile; extraordinary even, notwithstanding being well aware of our limitations.

David says that his childhood stutter "lived on in me for many years, making me always doubt my ability and worth". Yet he went on to set up and lead a fine Christian Counselling Service in Gloucestershire. What can we learn from this? This book makes that very clear. If we follow God's leading, He will provide us with all we need. The wisdom, love, patience, determination, stamina, inspiration, encouragement ... the list is endless. As David says, God provides us with those on the journey from whom we can learn, those with whom we can laugh and cry, and those who will pray, those who will support. As you journey with David through this book do look out for what God is saying to you.

Author's Comment.
David Depledge was one of the pioneers in Christian Counselling in the UK, and has been involved intimately at the helm of ACC for over twenty years.

Foreword
by Revd David Bick, Christian
Counsellor, Spiritual Director

Author of "Let your Faith grow"

When I first became aware of the contents of this book, and gave time to praying and thoughtfully reflecting upon them, my mind was directed towards the words of St. Peter as recorded in his second Epistle Chapter 1, verse 16 "For we did not follow cleverly devised myths when we made known to you the power and coming of our Lord Jesus Christ. But we were eye witnesses of His Majesty" Peter's statement refers to his experience of Jesus on the mountain at what has become known as the Transfiguration. Peter just told the truth about Jesus, as he witnessed it for himself, not speculating about some fanciful religious theory. I think that David Walker is doing the same. He is giving honest testimony to the way the risen Lord Jesus Christ is at work today in his life, and in the lives of many others with whom he has worked in various capacities, amongst whom I would include myself.

The statement I have just made sets David's book in the context of a very sound and historically based tradition. This tradition from the time of St. Peter until today demonstrates through experience the activity of the Divine Presence in the day to day lives of those who commit themselves to follow Jesus Christ.

This, as I well know from my own experience, is a reality that needs to be demonstrated. This is what I see David Walker, in his own way and from his own experience, doing very well indeed.

David was nurtured in Methodist homes both in UK and USA. I have read his father's book, called "The Church of Judas" and consider it to be a prophetic work. It points out some of the basic failures of the present day churches, in particular their inadequate spiritual nurture of the faithful. I say this as one who has read John Wesley's Journals, and fed off the words of Charles Wesley's hymns. I am aware that David Walker in describing these Christian families, has given his work the spiritual dimension that is truly rooted and grounded in Christ. This sound basis is so refreshing in a world of mass communication and clever technology, that so spreads distortions, falsehoods, hypothetical nonsense and confusion like a chill damp November fog.

Revd David Bick, St. Joseph's. Prinknash Abbey, Gloucestershire. September 2011

(Author's comment: For over 20 years David Bick was my Mentor, and like the title of his own book, I found my own Faith growing during our times of meeting together. That he came from an Anglican tradition, and was respected by Christians of all denominations, was particularly enriching.)

Contents

Preface and Outline

Part One -Through and beyond stormy seas

This book tells true stories of travelling through times of fear, pain and trauma, and moving on from feeling helpless and despairing, towards peace and wholeness. It is partly my own story, but more importantly I want to tell how others found peace beyond the storms of their lives, too.

My story begins in 1939 when people in Britain were being shaken by War. I was just four, and lived at home with my older sister and our parents. Our Dad enjoyed playing with us, and Mum was often there with her Kodak Brownie box camera clicking. Her camera produced our cover picture.

We all knew that God's real world had colour, and sometimes more black and grey. Suddenly there seemed to be less playing, more praying. Life changed dramatically. *"Will Hitler land on our beaches?"* It happened so quickly. For this little boy it was bewildering. We children were off on a big ship across very stormy seas to a colourful land called "America".

This is symbolic of the theme of this book. Life seemed grey – then BLACK. But because parents clung to their faith the Creator's true colours emerged triumphant, In God's good time. Looking back I found that life is often like that – if we can gain God's true perspective.

Parents waved us goodbye It was certainly no holiday when we began many days of constant seasickness! We were on one of three ships carrying children. Daily we "evacuees" practiced lifeboat drill. I remember being really scared as our ship was sent on ahead. "Submarines are coming" I did not know really what was going on. It was cold. I remember the icebergs. My sister would rather forget seeing bodies in the water. ("Three of the sixty ships in the convoy were sunk.") My own scary "little boy lost" feelings went in very deep.

As a child I just felt overwhelmed by the changes which war brought. Trusting our parents, yet being separated from them. I could not feel safe or loved anymore. Those terrible fears laid foundations for the crippling stammer which dominated my life. The love I found in USA was different, and eventually I learnt to trust our new family, and the God to whom they turned. He did carry us through! The foundations of faith were laid slowly, only understood simply.

In future years I grew towards a faith which reached out to this God who was there despite the chaotic and bewildering childish feelings. In this strange new land my relatives showed us great Love, and really lived out the motto **"In God we trust"**. **We survived the War – and so did our parents – and sure enough our mother collected us and took us back to war-torn England in 1945.**

With hindsight, I know that our parents had shown great sacrificial love, immense faith and total dependence on God. My father was a pastoral counsellor, before anyone used that title. I had often wondered what happened in his study, but knew that people found peace by visiting him there. Slowly I too learnt to lean on his God. after many years. As the years went by, each person, each test, helped me mount the steep learning curve of life. I was enabled to grow through and beyond the difficult times and to find a new sense of direction.

Nothing that I did in later life would have been possible had God not heard my desperate cry for healing. Even though people thought I was mad to change to less well paid jobs for more job satisfaction. Mary encouraged me to do so. At every turn God seemed to be guiding, even though we had no clear idea of what was the route ahead. The journey was fun, and amazingly creative. Friends seemed very special for us both. Those people from whom I learnt were amazingly first rate tutors in each of their professions. It was as if He had planned it all!

Therefore ....

This book has been written to describe the discovery of God's healing power. We were led to seek His Way by enabling others to experience it also. Everyone's journey has been unique, and ours surprised us at every step. Along that Way we seemed to be guided by wonderful travelling companions, many of whom were pioneers in the new Christian ministry of counselling. This was the time of our lives when we felt most fulfilled in every way.

Part Two   On Probation

So, although I had been a rebellious teenager I found myself helping young offenders. Changing from well-paid retail management to Probation and Prison work was costly, but thrilling. The skills which I was learning prepared me for work in caring and counselling, towards which I now know God was leading me. It was as if He was saying "There I told you it would be Good". "I did not design a grey world and it was!

Little did I know then, but God was teaching me to listen to hurting people and, most importantly, to Him, Together we grappled with difficult new work, and found ways of helping people change their life-styles, *when they wanted to.*

Part Three   Beyond it all.

Together, towards a Christian Counselling Service. This was a time when God seemed to be preparing so many to be His people helpers. I was not the only one who had been healed, only to find my self ending up in the healing ministry. From that moment I found a new freedom, new colourful vistas opened. He took me out of my childish bondage of fear and gave me a new Peace and sense of purpose. That is the story I want to share. As you read, please ask what this tells you about your life. He can bring new colour and HOPE to your life too!

He put me "On Probation". In 1977 it was back in Columbus Ohio, next door to my aunt's home, that I came face-to-face with "The God of Surprises". God chose a recovering addict in

Columbus Ohio to challenge this English Probation Officer to "Walk with the Lord". From that moment my life turned around from being what John Wesley called an "Almost Christian". I trained as a Methodist Local Preacher. Then, whilst still in the Probation Service, in my spare time attended a course in Christian Counselling in Bristol. So this is what He was leading me to! The tutor was Roger Hurding (The British leading writer on Christian Counselling in the 1980s). He enabled the pieces of my journey to fit together. **I KNEW what God had intended.**

So I want to tell the amazing story how denominational boundaries were broken down as Christians realised common visions, and we began to plough fresh furrows with people of like mind. I am so grateful for being privileged to be part of similar pioneer teams of people in the Association of Christian Counsellors who have followed different routes to the same end. It was an amazingly creative adventure. This is where I was introduced to Rev. David Bick, a respected local Anglican Clinical Theologian, who became my mentor for the following 25 years. I needed his Bible-based wisdom; and to be "thrown in the deep end of ministry" by a Christian who happened to be a Methodist. For the past 30 years I have been fed by the "Everyday with Jesus" Bible studies of Rev Selwyn Hughes. This pioneer who founded the Crusade for World Revival - an ecumenical Christian counselling ministry. Beginning everyday by focussing in prayer helped thousands of Christians; and I was one who owes a great deal to this discipline and chosen opportunity to focus on God's path. I needed that clarity and vision, whilst learning to work with Listeners from the whole spectrum of Christian Caring locally. It was vital that this sort of new work was blossoming nationally. It was a great privilege to meet people of like mind from all over UK, through the Association of Christian Counsellors and later from many USA and Europe. Denominations became irrelevant as we worked together to follow God's common purposes.

People came to join our training, management and supervision teams whom God had already prepared with relevant training and experience. The same was happening in Coventry, Cardiff, Northampton, London, Essex, Blackpool and Scotland

and throughout the UK... Everywhere new services were springing up.

A rich fellowship was developing. I seldom asked what church people attended, except when I enjoyed worshipping in most of the 74 churches in Gloucestershire which supported our new work. **Together we grew in faith – and it was very good!**

So in this book I want to pay tribute to those pioneers. We learnt from our differences and always strove to achieve the highest "standards of excellence in Christian Counselling – and Pastoral Care." We held national conferences and shared ideas through the Journal "Accord" (which I was privileged to edit for seven years.)

Part Four   "Counselling on the edge".

We were in the business of helping people who wanted to change. In the next ten years we learnt new skills, trained some two hundred Christian volunteers to counsel, using ever-changing and improving courses, guided and accredited by ACC and (eventually) secular Training Establishments such as the "Open College Network". We were always seeking to improve what we offered.

In those pioneer days we normally counselled in one-to one situations in our counselling rooms, in the three centres which developed. Often people came who did not want "**Christian Counselling**". We never turned these away, and offered services similar to any secular counselling service.

In this book I have chosen to share nine true stories of lives of people who came for help in the pioneer days when sometimes we were on the edge of our growing knowledge. We counsellors often prayed together for guidance as we sought to help people who felt themselves to be on the edge of an abyss in their lives. In the stories that follow, the people were all "Christians". Because of the particularly difficult presenting problems, I chose to counsel these people myself, with a different counsellor on each occasion. We grew by learning from each other, and listening to "The Wonderful Counsellor". Each new challenge was enriching – and it has been wonderful to meet these people many years later when they each offered their stories for use in this book. It is their generous witness that best tells the theme of this book. What does their stories tell you about your struggles and their realised hopes? I thank them all for their generous witness. The ninth person has gone to be with his Maker. He told both of his counsellors individually that we could share his story before his death. In all instances we have changed names and identifying details in order to preserve confidentiality.

Part Five   The Family

It is vital to say how much I am grateful that my family have grown up so well, despite the fact that sometimes they must have felt mystified and perhaps even marginalised when my work priorities seemed to take precedence over them. That they survived so well is mainly due to the great support which my wife Mary has given throughout, and our agreed boundaries of confidentiality, drawn up in love. This was especially necessary when I was dealing with damaged people who had committed serious violent offences which had resulted in long prison sentences.. It was my daughter in law Tracey who finally said "you ought to write a book". So here it is. My hope is that readers will understand the constant revelation of the promise that

> ***"With God all things are possible for those who believe."***
> (Mark 9:23).

Part Six   So What?

Letting Go and letting God.

This final section is a brief reflection, which concentrates on the first 10 years that Listening Post was in operation, at the end of which I retired.

We are only called "for a season". That was a most important lesson for me. I do celebrate the pioneer work of members of the Association of Christian Counsellors, whose aims to be a ***"Catalyst for excellence"*** were realised across the United Kingdom, and in many other countries – notably in USA. Services such as Listening Post have continued to develop and thrive more than 20 years after Christians tentatively sat down to pray and devise how to implement the emerging vision which we shared. In the process we set aside our denominational labels and worked purposively.

TOGETHER.

Part One

"Duchess of Atholl" with evacuees escaping the submarines

Through and Beyond stormy seas

1. From happy families to shaky foundations

They tell me I was a weak baby -"not certain to live and needing to have special milk". My parents prayed a lot - and here I am 75 years later telling the tale. Miracles do happen. My Dad was a strong man; a Staffordshire Coal-miner who eventually trained to be a Methodist minister and married a beautiful "Button". Yes, that was her surname – and her family were tailors. If I tell you she was "bright as a Button", you will think I have a weird sense of humour. Well, I do have, just like my Dad. In fact I turned out to be a lot like him. My favourite photo says it all. There I am on Southwold beach aged 4 shovelling stones down his back. He is grinning and my Mum's Kodak Brownie Box camera clicking for posterity. Dad enjoyed me being a bit naughty like he had been. He recalled how, when he told me not to play with water in the garden, he caught me out waiting with little bucket under a kitchen drain-pipe to catch the drips.

I remember feeling secure until scary things began to happen in 1939 when I was four. People said suddenly "We are at war!" I did not know what was going on. I know now that Dad was just about to move to a place called "Lincoln", which was surrounded by airfields. "Would Hitler land there?" Little boy David was scared! Worse still, so were the grown-ups. Dad certainly prayed a lot. He told me later that he had written to his five sisters in USA " Please PRAY". Miraculously, these letters crossed in the post. Theirs said "We are praying" "Why not send your children here". So, like thousands of other children, big sister Averil and I were to be sent off –"to be more safe". Soon we were packing up to go by train to Scotland to get on a big steamer - the "Duchess of Atholl". With all the tears around, it was not much of a "holiday". (We were told that the convoy of sixty ships together meant it was "Safety in numbers" but that meant little to this four year old. Three of those 60 were sunk – but the "Duchess of Atholl" not until 2 years later).

I could only grasp was that I was leaving his Mum and Dad! That did not seem too safe! When everyone around us started being sick. They dished out life-jackets and we practiced on deck. It was certainly no new game – so horrible that some understandably prefer to forget it entirely. (That includes my big sister!)

When "submarines coming" was the anxious whisper – fear turned to terror. "Life-jackets on!" "Up on deck" "Those are icebergs up there!" So I stood on deck, wearing a life-jacket, surrounded by grown-ups being sick on a roaring cold sea. Grown up David can still remember the feelings.

"We're being chased by SUBMARINES". Probably adults tried to reassure. But that made it worse. I only recall those feelings little boy lost feelings, "left my strong DAD....my beautiful mmmmum." feelings. I clung to my toy monkey, Peter. Peter was scared too.

"Lovely Aunt Nell will look after you" they probably had said...I do remember being greeted by this cuddly lady with warm arms enveloping and exuding LOVE. There was this large man called "Uncle Albert" who wanted to be my new Dad. As we sat down to our first meal together Uncle Albert asked

British Refugees Reach Jerome

"What do you want for Breakfast my boy?"

"Ddddo you have – something like a heeeeegg" I stuttered.

(Uncle Albert often recalled this - even 40 years later. We both laughed)

To me he did represent the strength and reliability of my Dad. Uncle Albert was a miner like my Dad had been before being a minister. Uncle Albert was a Pennsylvanian hunter from the backwoods who sometimes disappeared for a few days and came back with two deer on the roof which Aunt Nell turned into bits of meat – bottled in kilner jars.

First British refugees to reach this district are Averil Walker (seated beside her brother David), who are being cared for by their uncle and aunt, Mr. and Mrs. Albert Reckner of Jerome, Somerset County. They are shown playing with their cousin, Joanne Reckner.

The family kept a newspaper cutting entitled "Refugees from England". Momentarily we were celebrities in Pennsylvania, being welcomed to little mining town, Jerome, near Johnstown. Eventually Jerome did become my "home". The five aunts were all Christians in the Church of the Nazerene - married, with their own children. Their obituaries (given to me in 2009) show how they are remembered with affection– even veneration – by members of that church.

My Aunt Averil was married to Herald Seese, a Brethren Pastor. who had a big lake near their parsonage home, where we rowed, fished and had fun. Aunt Nell's daughter, Joanne, was my age. We played and got up to tricks together. I was thus exploring a whole new world, still feeling lost inside, but aware of the love we were given. It was a big strange land. Uncle Albert showed me the Cherokee Red Indian Reserve. "Real Red Indians!"

Uncle Albert was the mine "Safety Man" Daily he went off to the "mine". He took us children there one day, down into the dark dampness. When he momentarily turned the lights off (and back on!) we felt FEAR… drip…silence….

Then we laughed with relief. In a strange sort of way this helped me to trust and rely on him. We began to feel secure again. Letters arrived regularly from home, and Averil wrote back, even broadcast once, confidently.

A big step forward for me was when I followed my big sister to begin school at age six, crossing scary coalmine railway sidings to get there. I eventually began to take on an American accent, but childish national loyalty made me not enjoy the ritual salute to "Pledge Allegiance" to the Stars and Stripes. Somehow I cottoned on to the fact that England had lost the War of Independence and one day I went home to Aunt Nell crying. She responded "You should be grateful my boy. Just think what America has done for you!" Aunt Nell often told me "For God so loved the world that He gave his only son that whosoever believeth on him should not perish - but have everlasting life!" "Now don't you forget that my boy." And I didn't. "That's what we go to Sunday school for." I still treasure the dog-eared Holy Bible with a beautiful coloured picture of Jesus washing His disciples' feet. On the first page she wrote :

"Presented to my only sweet boy David - Christmas 1943 by Auntie Nell." She told me "God brought you safely here – and one day your mom will come and take you back to England".

And she did, but only after we had moved again – to another mining town at New Lexington, Ohio. Yet more changes, new school, new friends. Nevertheless, it still felt like home, surrounded by love that gave feelings of security. The promises came true. Our mother did come to collect us. So, for two Walker children it was back to what would be the "new home" in Lincoln. (via one night on the 30th floor of a New York hotel and onto Cunard liner. "Aquitania", crossing the much calmer seas.)

It was very good to see Dad. Again he was facing more changes. We moved again from Lincoln to Hampshire where Dad had another new church.

We all had massive times of re-adjustment. England seemed to have massive bomb craters everywhere, especially in the Portsmouth Harbour area where we went to live. I realised something of the wartime horrors we had escaped.

I was teased for my accent – and my stutter, and sometimes because my Dad was a minister –

and I had the same middle name – "Hollis". They teased me about that and called me "Hhhhollis" I began to resent that name. Some of my attempts to get accepted in the peer group by some rebellious behaviour was a reaction to this. However, when I started to play soccer, and got quite good at it. I gained what today would be called "street cred". I was nevertheless proud to have been a little American.

My parents had my picture taken to send back home to USA.

"Across the pond" we learnt that Nell and Albert also had major changes in their lives. This was partially brought on by Uncle

Still proud to have been an honorary Yank.

Albert's mine being closed, rendering his 500 miners redundant. Strangely, their 5 years of fostering us two refugees had been good preparation for new careers as Child Care Officers. They ran a Children's home in Somerset County, Ohio and cared for many other needy children. To her dying day Aunt Nell remained an Adult Sunday School Teacher in a United Methodist Church.

Pause for reflection

I returned to USA several times in later years – never once having to pay my own fare (Which is just as well – as I have seldom had much money) In each of these trips "back home" some wonderful life-changing things have happened. In a Columbus Christian bookstore I discovered a tape and song-book collection. When I bought them back to England those songs served to encourage, bless and me – and also many other people in a life-changing way. We will return to this later – but one in particular became a theme tune

"He's still workin' on me – to make me what I oughta be" [7]

2.Through and beyond Crises to new home truths

Within a few months we were moved from east coast Lincoln to a "New home with Mummy and Daddy" in Gosport, Hampshire on the south coast. We were taken up on Portsdown Hill overlooking Portsmouth Harbour, which was brimming over with warships, newly returned from battle. There seemed to be more ships than water. I hated war and warships, especially the submarines. It was overwhelming. Peace and love were much better.

A reflective thought.

Is it at all surprising that a child, who has been through all those changes in early life, ended up stuttering? Today speech therapists would say that it was triggered by Post-traumatic Stress. The "little boy ddddavid" syndrome lived on in me for many years - always making me doubt my ability and worth...

One of the themes of my life's story is that I have become progressively certain that God has prepared me to learn the many lessons of life. This enabled me to go through and beyond traumatic life-changing events. This helped me to empathise with those who experience parental separation and trauma in their lives through crisis and change or broken relationships. God did carry me through and triumphantly beyond, so I can celebrate the sentiments of the song recorded by Elvis Presley and Jo Stafford in the 1950s: "It is no secret what God can do What he's done for others He'll do for you" [8]

In later life I devoured a relevant book about Changes and Crisis published by the Family Service Association of America in1965. "Crisis Intervention: Selected Readings– Howard J Parad Editor" [9]

In my later studies I drew copiously on a bank of personal feeling memories. These could be summed up in the slogan from "Crisis Intervention" that "All change is potential crisis, All crisis is about change"

3. Back home, Growing Pains"

So here was this stuttering 10 year old, American-speaking English boy starting afresh in Stone Lane Junior School, Gosport, Hampshire, England. I had never heard of "Soccer", or football as the English played it - but somehow I coped with teasing about my stutter and accent. English boys liked the yankie troops with their chewing gum, and Glenn Miller music. The break through into the peer group came when I began to understand English football. I found I could play well enough to get into the school team We practiced in the streets at night.

The Football team which gave 11 year old David (top right) some "street cred" with his English peer group.

My parents encouraged all this. Strangely, measles helped too. When the school team got into a Cup Final and the Headmaster called at my home to see if I would be fit enough to play and I could! The final was on Gosport Borough Athletics' pitch and I had "arrived"! Especially so when in my enthusiasm, I leapt into the opposition's centre-forward and gave away a free kick. We did not win, but that is how I earned some "street cred" from acting tough (when I felt far from it).The change of schooling was hard. However, I was not too worried because I was in with the gang - acting tough again. My Mother especially got wound up when she found a copy of a Naturist magazine among my belongings called "Health and Efficiency". (By today's standards this was innocent - but as part of my adolescent sexual exploration I did feel guilty about it)

Years later the lessons from this episode enabled me to learn something important both about myself and adolescence. Mum knew that I played tennis with girls, but did I do more? (In my fantasies I did! But probably it was good that the real developing person in me was actually very shy and timid) My parents were quite right to care about me getting in with lads who sometimes bullied. Once we bullied a teacher, which seemed fun at the time, but I felt horrible when he seemed to have a breakdown! Mum and Dad worried also that some of the lads were into sexual exploration. "What next?" They asked, accusingly. Reports of bad behaviour from school were concerning them.

4. The Big Boundary Moment[10]

It was here that my Dad drew a big boundary STOP line. When the school reported to him my involvement in bullying to him he gave me the ultimate threat, "If you don't sort yourself out my boy, you are going to Kingswood!" (Methodist Boarding School in Bristol) I knew even then that it hurt him to draw this line so firmly. He did not want to do it. I knew he meant it, but it was very different from sending us to America for protection. This was about my unacceptable behaviour. In my heart of hearts I knew it was fair but it evoked a real crisis which required changes of behaviour and choices – to be made by me!

"Little boy dddavid" felt insecure again. My Dad had spelt it out – He had laid down clear boundaries. With the benefit of hindsight I now see how difficult was the decision he took then. He said quite firmly "It is your choice! You can CHOOSE to act differently". That lesson went in deep for me. About this time my mother arranged for me to have piano lessons. Mum was a great arranger. With great practice and good intentions she sought to arrange people's lives. The kindness in her meant that over the years she befriended some really lonely people. She tried to sort me out a bit more. She knew I liked music, but could not see how much I feared the piano lessons. However, she got the message after six months when I preceded each lesson by being physically sick. It was not deliberate, but when she saw I could not cope with the extra learning and more seeming failure she let me stop.

Some 50 years later, after she had died, and I was aged 65, I chose to fulfil a dear ambition to learn to play saxophone and clarinet – and now I am delighted to play "In the mood" and "Fly me to the moon" and "Baby it's cold outside" etc in a 35 Piece Jazz band. "He will make everything beautiful in its time" [11]

Thanks to my mother I could still read music and learned to play the tunes I had long loved by Glenn Miller and other musicians, that I had loved for a long time. I was already becoming what is commonly called an "anorak" (obsessional collector) of Big Band and Jazz memorabilia particularly from USA.

20 years later I did visit Kingswood, but this time as a Probation Officer conveying naughty boys to the nearby Approved School. That was a lesson for them, and also a salutary reminder for me, as I recalled how my Dad had set boundaries for me - in LOVE. I had chosen to follow his way, but "There but for the Grace of God"[12] I might have gone the same way. It was a salutary lesson for me in both boundary- setting and empathy. In my subsequent Probation career, especially, I frequently had to recall this theme of how important it is to set firm and realistic boundaries – and not just for offenders. In counselling I continued to respect the principle to "Care enough to confront". Probably the counsellor could be the only person able to hold up a mirror to a"client", give accurate feedback and challenge. I needed that, and it helped me to have empathy for offenders who needed to learn these important lessons of life.

5. Making better choices

This boundary-setting made me rethink my attitudes toward peer group pressure. I struggled to gain acceptance and recognition as a person of worth – and so do a lot of young people. With a different group of friends we watched the then highly successful Portsmouth professional Football team play just on the other side of the harbour from our Gosport home. My Dad must have financed that. We stood in the same spot for each match. "Pompey", as they were called, became national champions two years running. We were thrilled beyond measure by this success! Sixty years on I am still a Pompey Supporter.

My hero was Jimmy Dickinson who played in the same position as me, and whose biography I treasure, "Gentleman Jim" [13] It is important for teenagers to have heroes, and Jimmy was renowned for seldom (if ever) needing to commit a foul. My hero played for Portsmouth 600 times and England 48 times.

In England Methodist ministers move frequently, and in 1950 we moved 100 miles away from Gosport to Ilford, in Essex. This necessitated another change of peer group, which I did find hard. It also meant yet another school. Would this change start another crisis? Well, at least it was for boys only!

Away from sibling rivalry and thinking I had to live in big sister's academic shadow. That was no bad thing for her or me. It is probably no surprise that both of us ended up in the caring professions, although we followed very different paths. Averil became a Jungian Psychiatrist. Her nine years work in Sobell House Hospice in Oxford enabled her to write the book "Facing Death".[14] I am rightly proud that this book, which is now in its second edition, has helped many people.

6. Nicer Challenges

As a family we never owned a car. We became known as "The cycling Walkers". While parents had "sit up and beg" bikes, I soon got a Raleigh racer and enjoyed cycling to explore the local Essex countryside – and beyond with the lads. It took a lot of courage on my parents' part to give me the freedom to go on a one week cycling tour at age 14, alone, round the Yorkshire Dales. My mother's sister and family lived in Kirkby Malzeard near Ripon. They introduced me to Youth Hostelling by enabling me to stay at their local hostel. This was a major step in my maturation. This was a physical and mental challenge, as I did cycle some 200 miles around very hilly country. It gave me a great sense of achievement, planning it, and then carrying it through. I wrote about the adventure for the School magazine. Eventually I was allowed to start a school Youth Hostelling Group with my peer group. This culminated in my organising, at the age of 17, a European Youth Hostelling Trip for a month, when for 6 of us cycled across France to Basle and down the Rhine to Belgium. It was extremely cheap and wonderful experience for all of us. In these days of so much more traffic and crime that would be more difficult, but it did give me a lot more confidence – and it was FUN !

More about choosing.

I now appreciate how wise my Dad was to give me the choice to go to a church where he was not the minister. In typical youthful cussedness I chose to stay at his church, Cranbrook Park! He thought I would gain confidence if I got on the stage and forgot myself in acting. My first big stage part was in an Easter play – I was the cock that crowed twice after Peter had denied Jesus three times! I sat there for ages waiting for my big moment of cocksure triumph – and crowed without stuttering! (Even now my walking group friends will make a request often in a wood) "Go on David – give us a crow"

Then I joined a group of young people called "Cranmeth", and I owe a great deal to them for putting up with my eccentricities and encouraging me to gradually mature through accepting some of their challenges. A lovely couple – Ron and Hilda Cass were our hosts. Ron, a Local Preacher, led our fellowship and fun – and we especially enjoyed the fun. Four of us wrote scripts for our "Glee Club" variety shows. They pushed me up front on several occasions. Once I played the part of American female opera singer "*Madam de la Grand Bouche*", giving a falsetto rendering of "Art thou troubled?" This brought the house down.

Then I was a Chinaman called "*The Ancient one*" who worked all day on the Great Wall of China "because I am up the wall". Neither character stuttered once!

Nerves and self-consciousness had gone completely whilst acting and making people laugh. I still have that silly corny sense of humour. I learnt to dream up a rapid pun, because as a stutterer I was always quick to seek alternative ways of saying words, and often that made communication easier. I am still crowing that my Dad knew a thing or two about people and about me! I began to have a few girlfriends and tentatively asked one Mary Gill to go to dancing lessons with me. Here we are on stage together. It gave us both confidence and we even danced together in the finale of one show.

The group put up with me going on about "my Economics master" who was very wise. When I thought I was not good enough to apply for University, they persuaded me to have a go at applying even though it was after all the closing dates for applications. So I yielded to peer pressure, applied to seven Universities "just for fun", and amazingly I was accepted by London School of Economics (and several others!). It does seem to me to be uncanny how God seemed to know just what I would eventually end up doing best, to prepare for what lay beyond.

That sounds very much like boasting but St. Paul says in several places that it [15] is OK to boast about what the Lord has done – and I do that often with Praise."With God all things are possible" [16]

7. The "Ephphatha" breakthrough

I loved the wonderful Library at LSE and learnt speed-reading, so that amazingly I was able to extract the meat from several books or articles each day [18] I found that when a person sits down to write a book he or she has something they believe is important to say.

The best lesson I learnt in life was that God helps you most when you are down and when you reach out to him, He LISTENS - and wants to heal. For me it was really life changing.

One day, when I sat in the library at LSE and got really depressed about how impossible it was to be in that goldmine of learning and not to be able to ask for a ticket home to iiilford... (I could not seem to say aaany word beginning with a vowel)

This thought drove me into a telephone box in the street outside in floods of desperate tears and I cried out to God to "HELP ME PLEASE"

That was my "Ephphatha" [19] moment. Somehow I knew God had heard my cries. Many years later I read William Barclay's description of this wonderful; moment, "***Jesus looked up to heaven to show that it was from God that help was to come. Then he spoke the word 'Ephphatha' 'Open up' – and the man was healed.***

Don't ask me how, but within days I did not stutter!

I remembered that Jesus said "Ask- and it will be given" but I had never [20] seriously believed he would do it. This time I was like the woman who had bled for 18 years and came trembling to Jesus. She dared to reach out and touch the hem of his garment. I also dared to reach out. I did cry out. I did ask God desperately - and He heard and healed. [21]

Without this I could never have done any of the things which I celebrate in the later chapters of this book – teach, preach, or counsel. He was again preparing the Way. That is why I belief in the healing power of Prayer.

Aunt Nell could have sung "It is no secret what God can do

What he's done for others He'll do for you"
("Now don't you forget that my boy")

8. Dancing lessons – a new partner and more new dances.

For the first year at LSE, I studied mainly Economics-related subjects - and then spent two years specialising in Sociology, Psychology and Criminology. In future careers I needed all these subjects - but had never contemplated them when I applied to LSE. It seemed that once I allowed God to influence my choices, He got me on His wavelength and my choices began to shape up to His plans. It seemed that a lovely girl called Mary Gill, whom I had known through Cranmeth Youth Group would soon become part of those plans. Although, shy little me could not pluck up the courage to ask her to go out with me, I did ask her to go to dancing classes. She agreed and we learned about each other to strains of 78rpm records of Victor Sylvester's waltz and foxtrots. We also made rugs. While her maiden great aunts watched us, we sat on their settee and worked towards each other making rugs. We were dab hands at rugs! (Better than our dancing!) When we got to bronze medal standard we did not need the dancing classes and knew enough to realise we were in love, so we got engaged. In fact we danced at Mary's 21st birthday party – and got engaged when I was 21.

Our shyness had worn off and we could stop going to dancing lessons.

Mary waited for some four years for our marriage – as I had to do two years' National Service. Progress was slow slow – knit knit slow … I resented that wait - but decided to make the best of it. Against all odds I applied for the War Office Selection Board – to train to become an Officer. When the three days' tests came, I threw all caution to the winds . The assault course would be my biggest test. A rope hung in the middle of a wide stream and we were told to run and dive for it. I could not swim and (need you be told?) hated water! The Sergeant Major said the momentum would carry us over. I thought - "to hell it will" and just ran flat out... dared to dive... and Lo and behold caught the rope... seemed to fly and landed on dry land! Suffice it to say I was possibly the world's most unlikely soldier, always in trouble with the Guards Sgt. Major.

Wonder of wonders, I started as a Basic Training Platoon Commander at Hilsea Barracks in dear old Portsmouth. When the Battalion Messing Officer got sacked for getting the finances in a real mess, they assumed that with B.Sc. Econ I could at least sort that out. After a two-week's course at the Army Catering Corps Training Centre I found myself in charge of the food of 1000 men. In my wildest dreams I could not have imagined having such a position of responsibility. However, thanks to a wonderful Staff Sergeant and imaginative recipes, the troops survived our catering– and even sometimes told me they enjoyed it!

Great-uncle George loved Mary, but had great difficulty in showing it. He had a hard life as a foundry owner, and wartime warden, and died of cancer very painfully. The lovely Great-aunts and had kept a protective maternal eye on Mary and now they approved of our marriage!

Three days after demob, the waiting time was over. On 25th July 1959 at Cranbrook Park Methodist Church, in Ilford, my Dad conducted our wedding. These maiden ladies had a life of fulfilling their maternal instincts through two successive generations, as Mary's grandmother had also died in childbirth. They had brought up six other children before taking on Mary as a baby. Auntie Alice died within two weeks of our wedding, and received her reward in heaven.

We set up our new home in three furnished rooms in Ilford. John Churchill, my friend from LSE and the Army, was my best man. This part of the story seemed complete. We both married and started new lives in separate careers. He and I had been close friends, but sadly we lost touch with each other. However, 48 years later he tracked me down via the internet and it was wonderful to recall the friendship, which had been important to both of us. He settled in his native Wales and most recently became one of the historians of Coity Castle near Bridgend.

9. A new life began – together.

On my discharge, the experience as a Messing Officer got me on a Graduate Training year with J. Sainsbury Ltd, one of UK's leading grocery retailers. I then spent time in each department (including the Directors' corridor) and I soon learnt that their reputation as the leading Grocery firm in London was well justified. I soon worked in most departments, including their factory making pies and sausages, the buying sections, and even attending meetings where major policy decisions were made. It was then a real family firm, with jealously held high standards, Finally I worked in the Warehouse and Transport Section at a crucial time, when their distribution system to 240 stores was being decentralised. Sainsburys were one of the first UK retail grocery firms to introduce computer- generated distribution systems, and we were proud to be pioneers and innovatory in many ways. I still shop at Sainsburys and believe them to have the highest standards in all respects. The company sent me on management courses, and seemed to approve how I managed my seventy men and thousands of products. Prospects looked great!

Soon Mary enjoyed exploring a variety of temporary secretarial jobs. We bought our first house in Surrey a few hundred yards downhill to the railway station– direct into Waterloo – near

Sainsburys head office and warehouse – where I worked! The pay and prospects were very good....! We settled into a Methodist church near our home and gained friends. We liked living in Stoneleigh,Surrey. Although we had been disappointed by two miscarriages, at last our first beautiful child was born - "Teresa". What a relief and JOY! Aunty Betty came and proudly held the new baby – and my mother was there too - with box camera poised!

I changed my motorbike for a Morris Minor car. We had seemingly "arrived"!

HOWEVER, the "Lord of sea and sky" did not let us get too comfortable. I was promoted and appointed Manager of one third of a new distribution depot in Basingstoke responsible for distributing all of the non-perishable goods to seventy Supermarkets. This meant having 70 staff under me on three shifts six days per week. We moved to a new bungalow in Kingsclere nearby in what seemed to be an idyllic village of Kingsclere. It was an upheaval after only a couple of years in Surry, but it seemed to be confirmation of the promise in this management career. We soon had the added joy of our son "Stephen" being born. My Dad wrote to Mary when he got the news - "The top buttons burst off my waistcoat". After pain of disappointments came the joy of new birth- again!

There was my mother on hand watching proudly as young Teresa gazed in wonder at her new baby brother We lived on a new bungalow estate with young families like us. Mary and with her new- found soul-mate Di started the village Wives Group. I was led to start a Youth Club in the Methodist Church in my spare time. We also had a youth "Squash" in our home on Sunday evenings. I enjoyed working with these young people – and often found that they came to me with their problems. They seemed to trust me – and I found new feelings of satisfaction in helping them.

Mary had a wonderful few years as she was able to meet and then correspond with her father. This helped them both, and we visited him and his relatives in County Durham. This filled many gaps in her family history. Sadly he died after some five years, but she can still treasure some 400 pages of letters from this very intelligent and wise man.

My job went well and I coped with the problems presented by shop stewards and directors. The stores received the right goods and staff seemed content. The future seemed assured, but somehow I knew that was not the final sort of work for me. It paid very well. My future was mapped out, and after the arrival of our little boy Stephen we were settled and happy. My parents then retired to the village, and for the first time in their lives had their own little cottage!

The Queen's horses were trained there! Not only was my mother "snap-happy" with her Kodak Brownie camera, she did a watercolour picture of the Queen's horses in the village – and the Trainer recognised them.

We loved living there. Why change?

However.... It was my spare time work in the Youth Club in which seemed to be enthusing me more than ensuring the regular supply of food to stores. I found the challenge of engaging with these young people and helping them through minor crises was more what the LSE course had prepared me for. Why on earth had I read all that Psychology and Criminology, if I would never use it again in my work? I had not realised how much that learning had impressed me. My own feelings of brokenness through National Service, enabled me to identify with people who experienced despair and unhappiness. Now sometimes I met it in others in Youth work – and found that what I later called "empathy" – and this helped me to understand – and help them. I even took an evening course as a Hampshire Youth Leader, which felt good. I knew that the people I met at work also had problems - but I could not help them. The object of management was to ensure goods got to shops, and if I saw personal problems these just had to be left. Mary saw how much the youth work enthused me, when our home was filled with young people on Sunday nights. I never thought this out clearly, but when I saw an advert for the Probation Service it rang bells. The words seemed aimed at me, but surely only an idiot would leave such a well-paid job!

Nevertheless this niggling thought had taken hold and I had to admit to myself that probably a person-centred job would really have given more job satisfaction.I realised that the salary would be less than a third of my current pay – and even less for the first year of training; so, with a sigh I stuffed the ad in a drawer without telling Mary. Lesson number one - never do that when you have a tidy wife! She knew that in reality some of the pressures and grind of managing such a big project on a round the clock were often getting to me. She detected that some of my sighs represented the fact that the job was squeezing the time available for spare time youth work where strangely I felt more personal satisfaction. Mary had already realised that and read my mind. Then, when she was tidying up she found the almost disgarded advert. "You want to do that, don't you? You really love working with young people" "But we can't afford it, with two children and a mortgage." I protested. "You've got nothing to lose by making enquiries. If that's what you really want, and you think it's God's will then let's sleep on it. We'll get by and the money does go up after training...." (She had been reading the small print of the ad...)

I went to bed praying about it – and woke at 4am knowing that God was to move on. In the years that followed, I do seem to be woken often at about 4am – and on many of those occasions God seemed to be presenting some challenges about change. Change as adventure – The real meaning of "Partnership". So we decided that I should apply for Probation Training in London, where I was interviewed by Home Office Inspector and Trainer, Herschel Prins. Clearly he was checking out not just my ability - but more especially he wanted to know why I wanted to change from such a good job. (By implication - "Is this man sane?") He made it clear that Probation was not Youth Work – even though he saw I enjoyed that. He wondered how I would cope with hardened crooks or rebellious youths; sex offenders or alcoholics? Bank robbers or child abusers? I found myself saying that I believed most offenders must have had disturbed childhoods – and gone through many crises in their lives – and they needed at least "A Second Chance". That book's title described the aim of Probation and it only made me more determined to apply.

10. A Second Chance? Is it madness or golden togetherness?

Mr. Simon Sainsbury (Personnel Director) had written to me, wishing me well. He gently apologised for the fact that, because I was leaving, he could not give me the £300 per year pay rise I might have expected. (I was receiving over £2000 pa – which in those days was excellent money – when our new bungalow had only cost £3,000!) When I went around Stamford House Headquarters, saying "goodbye" most people declared me "mad" to leave, just when my prospects seemed so good. My reply was always that, although I would always hold "JS" in high esteem, I felt called to different work. Mary appreciated that – but others at work shrugged their shoulders in disbelief. I could never have made those giant steps from security and step out into new territory alone. We had to be of one mind. Mary has always been my encourager and support and for that I have been eternally grateful.

A pause for thought about what makes a good marriage.

Mary and I are very different in family background and interests, but we share values and Faith and Love. We still complement each other in things that matter. Every time we use the set of fish cutlery which my landlady gave us I remember her kindly meant words of doom **"All the best to you both** " *(aside)* "*It will never last*". She knew us both well. When I gave her a box of chocolates with two dud hard sweets she did laugh – eventually. She gave me great lodgings, and she saw Mary's love of classical music and mine of Jazz as symbolic . We may have tripped over each other in dancing classes but in the dance of life, we are still enjoying the cutlery 50 years later! The age of miracles was definitely not past !!!

Mary had been bombed out three times – and her mother had died giving birth to her. The love of two maiden great-aunts and a single great uncle had nurtured her. We were both survivors – but joined together in wedlock…God had enabled us to rise beyond low self esteem and wartime trauma.

We have moved on in love through a 50 year marriage – which still flourishes beyond our 2009. Golden Wedding. So we celebrated 50 years of living down my landlady's doom-laden predictions. We slept in one of the late Beatrix Pottter's four poster beds in Yew Tree Farm in the Lake District ("obviously with new mattress " Mary adds). We admired Beatrix Potter's imagination and resilient determination to protect the environment she loved. I had gone very unwillingly with Mary to see the film "Miss Potter"[22] but here we were spending a wonderfully memorable week visiting most of the 14 Lakeland farms which this amazingly generous woman donated to the British National Trust - thereby being a joint Founder of that organisation. This most talented of ladies, died in 1943 (when we were both aged 8) but we are among those who celebrate her generosity towards children and our environment.

So that ends Part One.

We had put God in control, started a family…I had a steady secure job with a great future; until another 4am call – and the Probation adventures started **Was it all a mad moment – or a God-given Adventure? We decided to obey God's Call.** In faith we launched off into new territory. Was I going in at the deep end? When I got my first taster with a three month orientation placement with a lovely Probation Officer in Banbury, Oxfordshire – he showed me that this was a life I could enjoy.

Mary kept the Kingsclere home base going whilst I flitted off on weekdays to learn about the new life. I reported back at weekends – then spent the second three months soaking in the theory of the Home Office Probation Course, based at Cromwell Street, in London. We survived on £650 pa…

So this was Probation! And it was good

Part Two

On Probation

In 1876 the first Police Court Missionary was appointed to Southwark and Lambeth Courts in London "for the purpose of dealing with individual drunkards, with a view to their restoration and reclamation".

By the 1907 Probation Offenders Act was introduced "to enable the courts of justice to appoint probation officers, to pay them salaries or fees. 124 male and 19 female missionaries to police courts were already in place so that certain offenders, whom the courts did not think fit to imprison might be placed on Probation under supervision. The duties of the officers was "to advise, assist and befriend". "Good quality practice" was that which seeks firstly to identify the real causes of offending, to empower the individual to bring about lasting change in her or his circumstances and to find out ways to influence the external factors contributing to her or his behaviour, carried out in a manner which respects the freedom and dignity of the individual at all times. "NAPO Practice Guide 1995[23]

11. Banbury Cross

The Home Office provided some excellent Tutors for me who greatly helped me to make my transition into the Probation Service. Working with offenders in a court-based service could have been a great shock - but as I followed the Officer in Banbury through his daily routines, met his caseload of sixty, read their copious files, and visited some at home and some in prison. I immediately felt excitement and assurance that this was the job for me. Every day was filled with new insights and challenges. I am annoyed with myself that I cannot remember the officer's name - but I do recall that "Mr. Bamford" (as I will now call him) was a perfect role model, respected as a professional by courts and clients alike. He spent much time emphasizing the sensitivity of "Confidential" material which affected people's lives, freedom and self esteem. He gradually gave me experience at a rate which I could assimilate – and allowed me to have a small caseload of my own and gradually write a few Court Reports, under his careful tuition. It was such a good foundation for which I remain most grateful. As I saw the work unfold before me I read "Casework in Probation" [24] by Mark Monger. This book written by the senior lecturer in the University of Leicester School of Social Work became a "classic" because the author acknowledged that literature on Probation was almost non-existent on this "new profession". "Bill" Bamford spared time to explain everything carefully and I quickly felt at home I wrote the Social Enquiry Report on my first "client". Going to his home was an eye-opener. Here was a man who kept reptiles in his upstairs sunny bedroom – and who had scared a crowded Unemployment Exchange waiting room by taking his five-foot pet lizard for an outing when he "signed on". That was not his offence. He was not the brightest resident – and had not realised that his pet was less loveable to others. What brought him to court was petty theft, not for the first time. The magistrates read my report and decided that this "rogue" should be not be sentenced, but put on Probation for a year. This was his "second chance"!

That was just the beginning. How would he respond? This depended very much on the offender's willingness, and ability, to change. In writing that court Report I found myself trying to assess that, and it was to be a constantly recurring theme of Probation supervision. Crisis theory suggests that the court appearance heightens motivation, as does the possibility of a prison sentence. Often when the offender has someone [25] interested in him perhaps for the first time in his life, this increases the possibility of a positive relationship which makes change possible.

If the court intends to make a Probation Order, the Chairman or Judge will ask the defendant whether he consents to the making of the Order, and to the Conditions in it. These would include the necessity of notifying change of address, to report to the Officer as directed, and to "lead an industrious life". There might also be requirements to accept treatment (eg for addiction) or to attend a Day Centre. If the offender agrees to these conditions and does not keep them then it is possible for the Officer to bring him back to Court so that he may still be sentenced in any way that could have happened originally. This gives some initial incentive for the client to co-operate. So much depends on the relationship which develops between them, and the aim for supervision is to encourage the offender to take this "second chance". For the first time perhaps in his life he is offered someone who cares to listen to him, encourage him, and also to set down some reasonable boundaries. During my time in Banbury I did experience one breach situation where the officer had his probationer brought back to court for not keeping the conditions, and he was sentenced for the original offence. The Officer offers a helping hand but also provides structure to a life which was perhaps chaotic. This was certainly true of the lizard-owning man mentioned above. I learnt to observe carefully, particularly on home visits. There were clues to his relation-ships with people – and the lack of warmth in his wife (whose teeth were kept in a jam jar on the mantle-piece.) was possibly echoed in his love of reptiles. Nevertheless, his wife did count it a small triumph for Probation that the Condition in the Probation Order that he "lead an industrious life" resulted in me helping him to grow vegetables – and find a job as a gardener.

As I read the records of my supervising Officer, I saw how he succinctly described each meeting and did quarterly summaries which indicated agreed aims for the Probation ahead and prog-ress. I attended Case Conferences with magistrates and heard the officers report on the progress of those under supervision. Also each team of Officers had a Senior who would review the work of the team. I began immediately to see that officers could handle large caseloads and understand many family situations, by keeping good records and working in a disciplined service with good systems.

In those days Probation Officers had a varied workload – which could include Juveniles (under 18s – which reverted to Social Services in 1969), the After-care of prisoners and Young Offenders ex- Detention Centres or Borstal, or Approved School. I was introduced to the wide variety of work - and the same dis-ciplined approach to records and supervision assisted my man-agement of large caseloads. Each officer in that team had some 60 cases operating concurrently at any time, so it required good time management and prioritisation. It also required good rela-tionships with families as well as the nominated "clients" – and home visits as well as evening and day office reporting ses-sions. I was glad to have such a good role model and he taught me well about prioritisation – Including working to shared tar-gets – and the possible early discharge of orders as agreed by the Magistrates Case Committee. These meetings showed me how these figures of authority were really interested in the progress of those whom they had sentenced. At the conclusion of three months I was extremely glad of such good introduction to the work which I went on to enjoy for 22 years.

12. Home Office Training

And so on to the Home Office Training Centre at Cromwell St, London, where I was privileged to have the man who had interviewed me, Mr. Herschel Prins, as the main tutor of the Course of intensive theoretical study. This built on the Criminology and Psychology that I had studied at LSE and took it much further. Indeed the Psychology which LSE taught me had been very much more Behaviourist in orientation (more about intelligence and personality inventories etc) so I needed the subsequent emphasis on Psychiatric explanations which the home office Course offered. I do not want to "knock" the Behaviourist theories, as in later years I came to value many different schools of psychotherapy and counselling. I learnt to be selective and realise that no one school has a monopoly of knowledge. Indeed, Hershel Prins encouraged that openness and questioning approach to learning. Nevertheless, whilst the LSE course gave an overview of the works of psychiatrists such as Freud and Jung, it concentrated more on the writings of people like Hans Eysenck – who wrote books like "Sense and nonsense in Psychiatry" [26] in a rather dismissive way. Under Herschel Prins, one book which I still own, and have frequently referred back to, was required reading "Emotional Problems of Living" ("avoiding the neurotic pattern")[27] by G Spurgeon English and Gerald H.J. Pearson. This psychoanalytical study of human growth and development deeply influenced my subsequent understanding of emotional problems. Many of these have deep roots in childhood and adolescent relationships Herschel Prins went on to write many books on subjects such as "Dangerousness" and I greatly respect him as a scholar. He sought to understand serious offenders [28] especially. His teaching, and the people whom he included as lecturers on the course, really built on the practical experience which Oxfordshire Probation had provided. These included legal experts, a psychiatrist from a large Epsom mental hospital; case workers and group facilitators conducting lectures and group sessions on the sort of practicalities we would meet in the practical placements over the final six months. There were some 40 students together, and 6 of us went on to train together in a Group under Miss Paddy Barrett for the final six months practical work in Hampshire. This suited me fine as I was able to commute daily to Andover from home...

Pause for reflection

A theme of this book is that somehow I was receiving some very good preparation for work which lay ahead. Things were moving fast in social work, and acquisition of necessary skills was essential. Although I was totally unaware of this at the time I do believe that God had His hand on my case. He provided the right experience and training – just when I needed it - Together with top class tutors and colleagues at every stage. In my opinion, the Home Office provided the best training available to potential Probation Officers. Eventually the course was succeeded by the two-year "Certificate of Qualification in Social Work" with specialist placements in either Probation or Social Services. The One Year ensured by group learning that theoretical factors were assimilated and then applied in court-based real situations. I was fortunate to be employed first in Hampshire for 15 years, where Paddy Barrett became one of the Assistant Chief Probation Officers. Hampshire Probation selected me for further training on two long courses which were a great privilege. I have always been very grateful to them for the unique opportunities they provided. The first of these specifically was specifically for Probation Officers. It meant attending groups at the Tavistock Clinic in London (one day per week for 18 months). This gave us insight into the unique psycho-dynamic ways in which this wonderful Clinic works. Anything which I subsequently practised which required and understanding of "Transference" issues stemmed from these wonderful sessions guided by a Dr. Goldblatt, whose knowledge and empathy seemed legendary to me.

Five years later I was seconded full time on the One Year National Institute for Social Work in London. This provided skills in Groupwork, Community Work, Management, and Training and Supervision. Buckinghamshire Social Services Training Section gave me two days per week practical work . All of this was invaluable when I sought promotion subsequently within Hampshire. However, none of these courses provided me with Certificates, but the new work for which they qualified me best is covered in the third and fourth pa\rts of this book. Pieces of paper may be valuable – but the real tests came in prison, court, counselling rooms and team meetings – or face-to-face situations with needy or hurting people. The Home Office Course was in itself more than adequate preparation, coupled with courage to tackle many new and potentially violent situations. "Feel the fear – and do it anyway" seemed a good motto! Slowly I learnt that there was Someone there who had called me – and who would equip me. Time would tell!

God knows!

13. Stepping out in Andover

So a group of six students joined the Probation Team in Andover – a market town in Hampshire, in size quite similar to Banbury, and covering a mainly rural area. From the outset we joined rotas for court duties, writing Social Enquiry Reports and accepting supervision responsibility for some six clients. Here we were putting the first six months' lessons into immediate effect. The difference was that Paddy Barrett used Group Supervision as well as individual sessions. This meant that we learnt from each other's work – and were able to grow together. Having the same theoretical base was useful in the weekly case discussions. It was a model which I used in later life when I had supervisory roles. We valued the presence of experienced officers and the support of the group as we tackled many problems for the first time. We also learnt about the community, its courts, magistrates, their clerks, social work agencies, police systems and personnel. Basically we discovered in detail how these fitted together in this town where there was much inter-agency co-operation. In later years when I worked on one of the country's largest council-housing estates this early good experience was a good model. It was helpful to study this with intelligent colleagues in group supervision with such a good facilitator.

I was particularly interested in a rehabilitation centre for drug addicts which had a Christian ethos. I was later able to compare that with another in Hampshire project which seemed to be equally successful in treatment terms, but which used a more behaviourist model of working. It was good to meet the leaders of these two very different units over several years, especially when some 8 years on the "Alpha" Unit conducted a Home Office inspired project which tested out the theory that "recidivist" (repeat) offenders were addicted to criminal activity as drug users were addicted to heroin. Such research fascinated me for, as I met more and more recidivists in prison and probation settings and felt strongly that these theories needed to be tested out. [29]So this six month placement enabled the theories introduced on the Home Office Course with Herschel Prins to be tested out under supervision in practice. It was an enjoyable process, and only served to convince me that Probation was indeed the career for me. The time came when we began applying for jobs around the country and I was accepted to work for Hampshire Probation Service, based in the area where my family had lived for four years after World War Two - Gosport and Fareham. We found a new house and prepared to move.

However, I had another big lesson to learn first. We were still living in Kingsclere, Late one evening a knock on the door revealed a Christian acquaintance with whom I had trained as a Youth Leader. We invited him in and over coffee he directed the conversation round to work with drug users. I remembered that he was a free-lance press reporter. I thought I was careful in what I said, emphasizing that any comments I made were from a very green knowledge base. He knew I was still in training as a Probation Officer. I was green in other ways too, for with hindsight as it did not dawn on me until after he had gone that he had been pumping information out of me. . (Mary reminds me that he was also a bee- keeper – and we did not realise what a busy bee he was that night. I should have told him to "Buzz off") My worst fears were realised when two days later the local newspaper had a leading article on the front page with banner headlines about the local drug problems. It began –

"Local Youth Leader and Probation Officer David Walker says...."

I was summoned forthwith to a meeting with the Chief Probation Officer, Percy Russell – and my supervisor, Paddy Barrett. They were both very angry. I thought - "That's my job gone!" My heart sank. I felt sick – and horrified at my own stupidity. I felt like a little boy caught with his trousers down – and almost bent down for the expected spanking. They listened to my explanations and apologies…and then expressed their disappointment in me allowing myself to be conned in this way. I did not lose the job – but **the memory of it went in very deep**. For many years I would not talk to a reporter – not even to say "good morning" in case he quoted the "good". I had prided myself on protecting confidentiality– and throughout my Probation and counselling careers never talked to Mary about any of my clients. The importance of this came home to me as increasingly I met, supervised and even cared what happened to some very violent, vulnerable and desperate people. The principle that people only should be told information that they need to know is paramount, and people will only trust you with their personal concerns if they believe you know how to handle the information they reveal. So I learnt early in my career that every professional relationship must begin with a clear agreed understanding of the rules and structures within which we will meet. In Probation, the Judge, or Magistrate will read the Conditions of the Probation Order and ask the defendant if he or she accepts those conditions. When consent to those Conditions had been has been agreed, then the consequences of failing to keep the Conditions were explained carefully. (In those days Probation was an alternative to sentence. If the offender did not re-offend and kept the terms of the Order, he would not be fined or imprisoned. But he could be brought back before the court and sentenced for the original offence. So there was a proverbial "arm up the back" to ensure compliance.

The Court and its Supervising Officer hoped the convicted offender would want to change his or her ways. The test of this would emerge during the period of Supervision. So at the first meeting after the Court hearing the allocated Supervising Probation Officer would go over all that in the first interview, set the guidelines for the one, two, or three years ahead. Very few offenders have sat down with one person and talked through an agreement – unless they have been on Probation. The very structure of this Supervision relationship gave to many their first experience of order in what often had been their chaotic and self-centred existence. Just to have someone who cared if you miss an appointment was new for many. For someone to ask you what you hope to get out of these meetings was equally mind-boggling.

14. "Changing Lives"

Working with offenders with structure was for me the norm thenceforward. We worked purposefully, gradually forming understandable contracts, some unwritten (or sometimes written but implicit). We were always seeking to help them to be motivated to change and to learn about boundaries which Society imposes, and the choices which are possible within the contracted time. A mutual trust had to be gradually built. At least quarterly the client and supervising officer reviewed our progress toward agreed aims. The officer wrote these in the records and kept notes of each meeting so these could be reviewed also. We worked towards eventual closure. These were really accessible and, in later years, the records became open to the client. Aims had to be achievable, discussed in detail with the client, and agreed'. He or she was not just a "case" even though I was using what was called then, "Casework". We were working together to help real change to be brought about. Hence the appropriate title of the history of the Probation Service – "Changing Lives". Note 30 These principles stood me in good stead for over forty years in different professional settings

"WOW!"

Pause for important thoughts.

It is 6am on Friday 13th August 2010 and I am sitting in my study thinking about my Dad. How amazed he would be - and proud – to see his boy David sitting with a Dell Computer typing stories remembered from 40 years ago onto a rewritable DVD to record important moments for a book. I am surrounded by memories– including some books re-read because they were amazingly important for me in my development as God has been "Workin' on me to make me what I oughta be".[31]My Dad died in 1966 – and he had been writing his book. He had been writing it in the feeling part of his brain for many years. He too used to wake up early and pray – "Lord, Teach me Your Way – help me walk in your Truth – Give me an undivided heart that I may love and honour Your Name."[32]

I can still smell the tobacco which reeked from his old type-writer. I remember, more importantly, his devotion to his God – MY GOD – that produced "The Church of Judas". [33] There are only about 6 copies of that book left. My mother had ensured it got into print, and Epworth Press had printed it for her. Curiously they had not dared to actually publish a book with such a pro-vocative title. My equally "undivided heart" must recall those feelings which are most important for MY book of my memories. My Dad, who loved God's Creation of our minds, would have rejoiced that his daughter Dr. Averil Stedeford had become a Jungian Psychiatrist and a Christian. He would have been especially proud (as am I) that she had written a book on her wonderful memories of healing through 9 years working as the Psychiatrist in an internationally renowned Hospice in Oxford .[34] So this book is my record of memories – and it was in a Hampshire town in 1967, 43 years ago, which saw me actu-ally sitting in a Probation Office, with my name on the door, with five experienced Probation Officer friends around me in Fareham. They nurtured me, taught me, pushed me into things which stretched and tested Me. I knew that this was the job God wanted me in. I was an "Almost Christian" [35] (As John Wesley called it) We went to one of Mr. Wesley's churches but my mind was undivided in excitedly drinking in real knowledge of strug-gling people, and I had a "patch" of two small towns nearby where I "cut my Probation teeth" with many families who were having a tough time. These colleagues of mine thought that I ought to take some of the least popular work (as I was just out of training), so I found myself being allocated all the court work and supervision of sex offenders in the surrounding area. I would learn best that way.

I did not mind, because as I sat down in one-to-one situations and visited the homes and tasted the ups and downs of their lives, I learnt what it meant to be brought face to face with the fact that a family member was in their local court for sex offending which had been going on beneath their very noses!

I got, at first hand, a taste of what deep feelings were involved – and what "empathy" was too! I had to stand back, remember my training, and realise that I could only help if I could find that necessary balance between being caring help in "Changing lives" [36] and objectivity during our contacts during the period of Probation. In August 2010 I have that record of Probation History on my desk – and I was a tiny bit of it – and proud that it was part of my story too. These people were hurting. When "the chips were down" at the time of trial, when they were being brought face to face with their shame and family feelings of ambivalence (love, hate, anger, despair) there were very deep feelings. Can you imagine a mother's horror that her little boy had exposed himself to other women, or a Chief Petty Officer's wife realised that her husband had "flashed" to a woman in a petrol station? And it was in tomorrow's local paper!

I will never forget the young man who was so jealous that his disabled twin siblings got all the attention in his family that one day he took all his clothes off and ran down the main street of his town. (In days when "streaking" was unheard of this was a heinous crime under the Vagrancy Acts) When the Court gave such men the chance of Probation I was the one to supervise them for one, two or three years. For a new Probation Officer, the "chips were down for me too"! I knew that immature men labelled as "sex offenders" could only be helped to change if their motivation was real – and at this point the possibility of helping was maximised. Although a part of me recognised that my colleagues were "dumping" on me some of the least popular and most demanding parts of their work – the people fascinated me. It was the family dynamics which appealed – and for which all the "Emotional Problems of living" taught by Mr. Herschel Prins had laid foundations.

I was very grateful. Suffice it to say that I found myself "grasping this nettle" and eventually ended up doing my own little bit of criminological research. I went over all the files of some 24 of my own sex offender clients seven years later to analyse the main causal factors in their lives. Crucially for them, and for my "research", I asked "How many had re-offended ?" My LSE days made me hesitate to draw too many conclusions from such a small sample. However, it was very pleasing that only one had re-offended (or at least been caught for re-offending!). So that was a great introduction to Probation work. I loved working on my "patches", The Council changed street names, to help de-label the people who lived there.

It was not very successful. I remember knowing that the whole street watched me going into the home of a prisoner's attractive wife – and how I deliberately talked to her standing near the window. I remember feeling vulnerable thinking "If I feel this way, how much more vulnerable must she feel when she takes her children to school". That was empathy! I enjoyed working with Prisoners' wives and families –with female Probation Volunteers – because they could always get alongside where I could not dare to go. Somehow the communities knew I was a safe person. That trust was vital. You get nowhere with hurting people if they suspect you have a hidden agenda. My own family were precious to me. I wanted others to treasure their own close relationships, with love and respect.

I never talked about my clients at home. It was VITAL to my work to draw boundaries, and this was fundamental to all my subsequent counselling work, especially when I worked closely with female colleagues. We work with strong emotions and relationships, which is delicate and precious territory.

15. In the deep end

I was often flung in at the "deep end", doing most work for the first time. Often we had duties which today's Probation Officers would not dream of touching – Voluntary Matrimonial Counselling, Debt Counselling and supervising "Money Payment Supervision Orders" where people got into debt by not paying fines. Two strong reminders of these times when senses and feelings went deep will give a "flavour" of how "cutting my teeth" taught important lessons. As in all subsequent descriptions of people I have carefully disguised identifying features and have invariably changed names. Where people have allowed me to tell their own stories I have gained their permission and asked them to check over what I am writing. We are dealing in this sort of book with personal confidential secrets which I have been privileged to share – and have responsibility to protect. I would have loved to tell many stories. When I have got to know intimate details of people's lives over sometimes three years, their hopes and the desperate fears which sometimes drove them to commit serious offences, I realised that very often they needed friendship and guidance to cope in Society. It would have been good to tell you about the young man whose terrible body odour caused the office staff to open all the windows when he was expected. I understood so much more about him when visiting his home and finding all the chairs covered with plastic. His seemingly pathological lying had begun in childhood when his mother had not been able to cope with his toilet training. He got into habits of lying about everything, and could not control his bowels at 20 years of age. I had to help him with some very basic problems! People often wondered why we bothered with such mixed up and immature people, but I warmed to their idiosyncrasies, and enjoyed helping them iron out the bumps in their lives, and find socially acceptable ways of living with what Society called "crime". – when they really wanted to change.

16. "Charity begins at home". Together with Love.

Love is the central thing in Christian Counselling - though that word is seldom specified in Probation training. A book which I learnt to value in later life is called "Love is a Choice" [16] and it tells many "home truths". We can help people to recognise and understand their relationships and to deal with the unhealthy ones in God's way. In Probation we met some lovely people – and also some whose learned behaviour made them not too nice to know. We learned to try to care about them and sought to help them to change, if they wanted to. In the next stage of my career I met even more people whose behaviour I simply abhorred. However, this book showed that I could choose to love, even those whose behaviour I did not like. Probation taught me about balanced caring, and how to handle the secrets people trust you with. They need to trust you to remember things that are vital to them. They needed to know that you never gossip nor giggle about them, even though you laugh *with* them sometimes. They also know that you know about their weaknesses, and will gently enquire about the sincerity of their promises to work at dealing with a tricky relationship. Each person can choose to face their hang-ups – or play avoidance games. In the privacy of counselling you and they get real about the important issues. I will return to this key concept ("balanced caring") and "accentuating the positives" however miniscule they sometimes seem to be. I always remember the theme tune of my USA childhood – Johnny Mercer's "Accenttchuate the positive, Eliminate the negative, Latch onto the affirmative, and don't mess with Mr. in-between" [39] (Aunt Nell used to add – "And don't you forget that my boy").

Working with offenders, and somehow helping them to get beyond the offending behaviour, means digging out with them those remnants of positive qualities which they can grasp hold of and develop – IF they choose to allow you to really engage with them meaningfully. Then the Probation will become time well spent. Perhaps the biggest lesson I learnt is that the "God of Surprises" teaches many lessons along the way. This certainly happened to me in Columbus Ohio in 1977 when I was on a visit. My Dad had visited his five sisters several times and after his death I took

Dad visiting his sisters   8 July 1962
May Brown, Averil Seese, Nell Reckner
Beatrice Plant, Lil Shaw

over from him. I really enjoyed living the American way for several weeks. One day I was invited to speak with the recovering drug addicts who lived next door to Aunt Nell. I thought they would be interested to hear about the English Prison and Probation systems. That was very naïve of me. When they walked into the room they were all carrying Bibles. One greeted me with **"Brother, do you walk with the Lord?"** No one had ever challenged me like that! I was speechless – and could not honestly answer

"Yes". I used to challenge addicts in Parkhurst to change, but here they were challenging me! They never let me go. They prayed for me. I went home shaken and very disturbed. Was I just a hypocrite? I certainly felt like one! I was trying to help offenders change their lives, and I seldom brought God into the equation. I knew that "With God everything is possible" and yet I could believe that Promise, but never acted upon it.

What a sham! Three days later we travelled to see three other aunts in Pennsylvania, and I shared with them how troubled I felt. They sat me down and prayed that the Lord would really take over my life. I found myself asking Him to "Teach me your Way" and determining that from that time on He would be my Guide. I thank God for those Christian addicts whose Serenity Prayer had so challenged me to know I was the one who needed to change, so I could then help others to change their lives *His way*. My prayer was *"O thou who changes not abide with me"*. He does! From then on I KNEW I must become a *CHRISTIAN* Counsellor and began increasingly to pray more and more about allowing God to guide me – and those for whom I cared. That night a quiet cousin of mine, Irene, whom I had never known well, gently knocked at my door, and gave me a

New International Bible to mark that momentous day. I still treasure it and the prayers she offered.

17. Pause for Thought. **About Mary Josephine Gill**

I want to add in here a bit more about Mary, whom I did choose to love as my Wife. She became more than a "Partner" (today's favourite title). I want to describe some of our own unique versions of "Love". You will remember that we met in "iiilford eeeeessex"– and she did not seem to mind my stutter. We grew up in the youth Club of my Dad's Church. Both of our families had firm Methodist traditions. "Love" is experienced uniquely in every family – and in individuals and partnership or marriage. We all learn what we mean by "Love" based on their own unique families.

Here are our different generational mixes.

Walkers and Buttons were surnames from my side; Pearts, Crowthers, Fishs and Gills from Mary's.

My mother's Button heritage came through her mother. My memory was that "Happy Victoria" Button seemed at times to be less than happy, but was victorious in surviving her own crises, when her husband and youngest daughter died within a year of each other. She was pregnant and the baby, "Beryl", spent years in mental hospitals in her troubled adolescence. Beryl had brain surgery which would not be contemplated today ("Pre-frontal lobotomy and leucotomy") yet she survived to be a lovely dear aunt – training to be a nurse, yet often requiring residential care in later life. I eventually had Powers of Attorney during the last few of her 80 years, and she left her brain and her body to be used for medical science.

As my family, we changed from prospects of wealth in our beautiful and settled family home in a bungalow and lovely village community. Relinquishing my job as a Manager in a growing and internationally famed retail firm, earning £2300 (a high salary in those days). This was hard for a young family with two children under five. In those days our lovely brand new three-bedroom bungalow only cost £3000. Mary tells me now in 2011 that in 1966 she did not understand what I did in any detail at almost any stage in my working career. She "kept the home fires burning" and provided our family with a firm base. That meant that the boundaries that I had drawn to protect her had been successful, in that I wanted my family to live peaceful ordinary lives despite my encountering turmoil at every turn in what was often an extraordinary job. I tried to minimize the attendant dangers in the work. This boundary was vital to my family. I see it more clearly now, and regret the pain that I may have caused by letting it float past me at times in my blind busyness. This was intended to protect but in my care for others I now realise that sometimes I must have seemed to give too little time to my family my family. This may have been my biggest failing in life, and for that I ask my family's forgiveness. I think that they now realise that I love them all dearly, and in my belated retirement I try hard to restore the balance increasingly. My only compensatory thought is that our generous God has given us many lovely friends at every stage who have sought to redress the balance.

It was I who gained job satisfaction working with offenders, broken lives, dangerous people. However, we had not envisaged how much the "crunch" would come in 1966. That year proved the peak of satisfaction for me, but the pits of depression for Mary, due mainly to the crisis brought about by too many changes simultaneously. In my job the realities were GREAT! At last I was with wonderful colleagues in the job I knew was for me, God-given. However, for Mary it was a great upheaval, and too many changes for one who had such an unusual and trauma-filled childhood temporarily overwhelmed her. The next few pages may enable you to understand some of our family dynamics – and I thank God for His protection and healing as we have tried to encounter each of the changes and crises in our lives with the sort of serenity that I later came to value through encountering the Serenity Prayer via Alcoholics Anonymous.[40]

(I hasten to add with gratitude that neither of us became anything other than tee-total as I know that for some under pressure, it is alcohol which is the comfort "blanket") Mary had a strange up-bringing with a much more traumatic life than mine. Her parents were very intelligent. Her father, Joshua Peart, was a product of an isolated village in County Durham called appropriately Cowshill, from which he was able to go by train daily to Grammar School ten miles away and became a star pupil. Almost a local celebrity, he went on to Queen Mary's College in London. There he acquired a first class Honours Degree and went on to teach German and French in a Surrey Grammar School. He met and married Muriel Crowther. She came from Forest Gate in London's East End. Muriel had been brought up with three sisters and a brother by two single aunts and an unmarried uncle who lived together. This family trio amazingly dealt with the disaster of their own sister dying whilst giving birth to Muriel by adopting the five children and bringing them up together. This was a family tradition of sacrificial love – which gave rise to my meeting the Gills and Fishes who have welcomed me into their wider family circle. Muriel was special to all of them – as she eventually studied at the Royal Academy of Music where she became a "Sub-professor" and married Joshua Peart. (I have touched on this dramatic story in Chapter nine). This young teacher was also a singer of German Lieder songs and they both loved classical music. Muriel won gold medals, composed music, had equally talented friends, and had a musical future opening out before her. It seemed to be a marriage made in heaven and soon to be blessed with a baby. On 30 May 1935 the Mary came - but after a difficult labour complications occurred and the mother was lost. Born into much grief, baby Mary was not claimed by the distraught father, Joshua. Eventually the two 60 year old great aunts Alice and Betty and the great uncle George (who brought up the previous generation when their mother died) claimed her after some weeks of deliberation. They eventually adopted her. Her mother's generation were thereafter a great support to Mary. However it was always very confusing time for a child growing up – especially when World War Two meant that Hitler's planes bombed out the family three times. On one occasion Mary had been sleeping by the fireside – and only the chimney of their house was left standing. One aunt was in hospital for a year. It is a wonder that any child survived such a bombardment in sound mind. Mary did, and eventually gained employment as Secretary to the Personnel Manager of the Eagle Oil and Shipping Company in London for many years. She was in that job during the time we began our courtship. Although Mary gained great stability and handled much responsibility in her work, and was great encouragement as a wife and mother, she did have the return of some reminders of difficult times in her childhood when we moved from the settled home in Kingsclere. She greatly missed her soul-mate Di and other friends there. My father died just as we started in Fareham.

We lived on a new estate and she did not quickly gain friends. The children were then aged 2 and 4 and they had measles so badly that she could not attend the funeral. She missed my Dad who had been a rock to her after his retirement to Kingsclere. Cumulative loss can be overwhelming. Mary had many difficulties just as I was starting in this new and demanding job. She had to seek medical advice, and was referred for psychiatric help, including group therapy in Southampton. All of this was unsettling for both of us. There were many emotional episodes for her. Individually some were very exciting. The greatest surprise was when she met her natural father, Joshua, for the first time. She was enthralled by his friendship. Somehow she kept her feet on the ground. As she made local friendships, Mary gradually regained her equilibrium. Teresa settled well into school. Having joined the local Methodist Church, Mary taught in Sunday School. We began to feel at home again. I am including this frank description of our own family background mainly to show what was going on "back at the ranch".

Sometimes we do not remember that workers in the caring professions have their own family pressures going on, and they have to make choices about priorities.

We learnt that "no one is fireproof". We can all be "wise after the event".

I learnt over the years to adjust my choices, and thank God for good colleagues, supervisors and friends for helping us through such times. In the end I can affirm that this painful period at least enabled me to empathise with many cases of family difficulties. I thank God that our love and shared faith saw us through. In consequence I have become a great admirer and supporter of the Christian organisation, "Care for the Family". [41]

Fortunately we did not have to make use of their services. but know how much their work is essential for many through times of crisis, and beyond.

18 God's Homeostasis - A Reflection.

"IF ONLY we had done the 1997 Mission to Marriage Course [41]at Lee Abbey in 1966" I have learnt, often the hard way, that God's timing is always right. We do have to learn by our mistakes and that I have often tried to do, although often belatedly. It does seem important to remember that we all have more than one theme going on in our lives at one time. Job, home, family, friends, church, hobbies, hopes, fears and memories run side by side presenting conflicting demands and emotions.

Somehow our systems seem to be programmed to find a new balance after each change. I have always admired the Creator's "Homeostasis" [20] – the rule of balance with which the whole universe survives and seeks balance. ("A cold gets better in a week – with treatment it heals in 7 days.") There seems to be a natural tendency towards wholeness as "God moves in a mysterious way". Two more changes were pending, both exciting. One was dramatic and challenging. My Probation Assistant Chief, former tutor, Paddy Barrett, appeared in my office one day and requested me to go to London on a course of weekly one day seminars for Probation Officers for 18 months at the Tavistock Clinic. This was a rare honour and privilege – and I could not refuse it. Mary again supported me going, though it meant more days without me popping in home for lunch.

I learnt so much from those times at the Tavistock Clinic' Doctor Goldblatt enabled us to grow in *empathy*, to *listen* with all our senses to the clients and their stories. We learnt to consider the dynamics in a four-person relationship, outlined in the Tavistock book "Shared Phantasy in Marital Problems"[42] I have re-read that slim book in 2010, and realise that the dimensions in that were helpful to me in counselling at several stages in my careers – even in 1990s in cases quoted in the fourth section of this book.! I will always remember Dr. Goldblatt tapping his stomach as he told us to "listen to your feelings – because however that person makes you feel has relevance to how he or she makes others feel".

Meanwhile, "back at the ranch" the home fires were being kept burning. I needed to be reminded that this God who called us to change is also the "God of Surprises". Paddy Barrett had just one more surprise to spring on me. She turned up in my office in Fareham, unannounced and said "David, We would like you to go to work in Parkhurst Prison on the Isle of Wight!" That is a prison for long term serious offenders. They had just had riots there. Throats had been cut. It was notorious. However it was a great learning opportunity. It was a possible upheaval for the family. We had to choose. It meant either moving to the Island or travelling daily. But there was another wonderful surprise in store. Strangely Mary had recently had a letter from a former colleague in the Eagle Oil Office in London who said that their friend Adrian Stanley, (who sat near Mary in her office for several years) – was in the Probation Service, Adrian had been in Coventry, then Winson Green Prison, and was moving to Hampshire! We soon learnt he was to be the new Senior Probation Officer in Parkhurst! It slowly dawned on me that Paddy Barrett was asking me to work under this man whom Mary had known well. It would be a great challenge. I had heard about the riots there. A new Governor had been appointed. It would an opportunity to work with this man who eventually became my closest friend.

Soon Mary and I were visiting the Island which we had often seen across the sea from our local beach. It was great meeting Adrian again. We remember how he tried valiantly to describe the beautiful views from the Island side of the sea on this very foggy day. He clearly wanted us both to be happy about it. There was no doubt in our minds as our two families met each other. Amazingly, Adrian and Katherine's two children (Mark and Rosamund) were the same age and sex as our children (Stephen 3 and Teresa 5). We have a memorable photograph of our first meeting. It seemed meant to be! Our families have been almost one henceforward. We had so much in common.

Once again – with hindsight I can see that God's timing was perfect. He was preparing the way – and when the crunch came for Mary to agree to my acceptance of the move, she acqui-esced readily. However, we both felt we could not move to the Isle of Wight, even though sunny Shanklin seemed very inviting and the children loved the sandy beaches. Nevertheless we did spend most of our holidays together over the next 10 years - on sunny Welsh, Cornish, and even Hampshire beaches. (Even walking the Cotswold Hills for over 20 years

I discovered that I could travel daily – by car, two ferries, a short train journey down the pier, and a second "old banger of a car" in two hours each way! It was possible, although it seemed to be a marathon. (I sometimes had to run the mile down Ryde pier to catch the ferry back, or catch a hovercraft instead). "Hampshire would pay all the fares." said Adrian, temptingly. "They must really want me to go" I thought with mixed pride and hidden trepidation, as reality dawned. Mary agreed I could do it – "If that is what you want!." Two months later, after a short course in Wakefield Prison, I walked into the famed Parkhurst Prison. As I crossed the exercise yard with Adrian, keys chained to me, I prayed an arrow prayer "O God! What have I done! This is pretty daunting, but You have called me......!"

19. Behind Prison Walls.

Everyone going into Parkhurst Prison goes through the little front door. It is daunting. This was my biggest challenge so far. There for 2 years From September 1971 I worked each weekday among men labelled murderers, rapists, arsonists, paedophiles, forgers, bank robbers – the sort of men that Herschel Prins had written so knowledgeably about. Mary fortunately recalls that I must have drawn the protective boundary quite successfully, as when I got up at 5.10 am each day and drove to the first ferry across Portsmouth Harbour, she never really had any idea what I would be doing.

One day as she stood in the bus queue with the children – someone from the other end of the queue shouted to her "How's David doing in Parkhurst??" That stopped the chatting in the queue! On another occasion two retired teachers got out some sweets for the children, mistakenly thinking she was a prisoner's wife. She could not tell them that each morning I said "Good morning" to murderers and sex offenders - because she had not added up the implications of the new job. Thank God for those thick walls – which did mean that as the door clanged behind me each evening I left my motley "caseload" of 100 safely secure. My main job, however, was to prepare most of them for the big day when they might re-enter normal society. That was an onerous responsibility – and a privilege.

I still remember vividly my feelings when sitting in the cell of one paedophile who was about to be discharged. No one could stop him going out. He had done his "bird" (as we used to call it). A Probation Officer from London had been visiting him every few months – and was seeking safe accommodation for him. The man suddenly decided to go to Wales instead. I quickly had to make Probation links there – just in case he carried it through. We all knew that wherever he lived he would prob-ably re-offend against a child. I shuddered at the thought. There was no Sex Offenders' Register then, but of course the police would be made aware. We just had to find ways of increasing the odds that he might not re-offend so quickly. The inevitable happened and we got news from the Probation Officer that he was in custody again. Fortunately our communications meant that our concerns could be transmitted to the Probation Officer who would write the Pre-sentence Report.

It was a fact of life that some addictions were so ingrained that there seemed absolutely no chance that some offenders would be able to change. This was the hardest bit of the job. The compensation was that with a few men there was a real, gen-uine desire to use the time in custody to make a fresh start on release. Many men lost all home contacts, or just needed to be released to a safe home in a different part of the country. It was here that we were able to plan with hostels, and home Probation Officers via "Aftercare" or, better still, "Through-care" to improve family situations. There was a Probation-owned hostel on the Island which provided family accommodation so that there could be extended visits over several days, and children could see their dad, There were Probation Volunteers who would look after the children while the parents talked things through, some-times with Probation counselling help. Such planned release maximised the chances of the emerging plans succeeding. When people who had gained the label of "Offenders" genuinely wanted to make a fresh start we could help them. There were some really good Christian charities specialising in helping prisoners to find new homes, and providing a friendly homely environment from where they could get help to find work, and even treatment for addictions. We got to know several of these, such as "Norman House" and the "Langley House Trust". This was started by a Christian called John Dodd, who lived on the Isle of Wight. Adrian and I eventually both had close links with this organisation, many years later, and I still value having news of their continuing ministry. (The wonderful story of Langley House Trust was published in 2010 [43] . This describes how there is help available when people do want to change and start afresh).

I was extremely grateful that my boss was Adrian, became my life-long closest friend thenceforward. He was truly my spiritual brother in every sense, and we grew to trust each other, and to debate and grow together. We were very different, but valued our differences. The values that we shared were more important than our varied chosen methods of getting there. Adrian was an innovative man who always looked at any problem sideways - and almost always came up with different solutions to problems from those offered by other people -as if by chance. Annoyingly I usually had to concede that he was almost always right. I came to call him, eventually,

"Mr. Serendipity"

We both came to believe that things did not happen "by chance" in Christ's Kingdom. However, whist I worked in Parkhurst, I was still one of Mr.Wesley "Almost Christians". [44] We seldom talked about our faith. All of that came in God's good time. (Ecclesiastes 3:11 – "He will make everything beautiful – in its time") Parkhurst proved to be my steepest learning curve, and I was delighted to have a former Social Worker from St. Martin in the Fields in London called John as the Assistant Governor appointed to be in charge of the Prison Wing where I was allocated to work. "Just by chance" we had adjacent converted cells as our offices. In the end I was given Parkhurst's first female Probation Student to teach (and protect) for three months. "Cilla" was brave to work in that almost totally male world full of serious criminals. She eventually fell in love with and married John the "AG". One day John called me into his office and showed me a photograph of the body of an old lady who had been raped and then stabbed 70 times. "The man who did this is our latest resident. I want you to interview him in a few minutes." Fortunately the picture was in black and white, I hated the sight of blood. That man straight away told me he was really innocent – "it was my wife who did it!" ("I bet she didn't rape her" I thought) I told him that I could only accept that a Judge and Jury had found him guilty and he would have to live with the fact that other prisoners would hate him because of it. I said that I did not do so – and it was my responsibility to be what used to be called his "Welfare Officer". "Welcome to Parkhurst!"

See what I mean about a steep learning curve? I was glad to have firmly decided to be clear about boundaries. Mary would not know about any prisoner. It was the "need to know principle" drummed into us on the Home Office Course. That I saw this man and others like him daily – even sat in their cells alone with them - would make Mary shudder. It took a while for the horror of that to sink in. I often needed that five-vehicle marathon journey home to unwind - and my peaceful little family to keep me in touch with "normality". However, this prison was the only available tangible world for those men, and it was our job to be part of the team that prepared them for a return to their other real world. Blood had been shed in that prison. I quickly learnt the rules to protect myself – and I valued the staff who kept us safe. Daily I held a sort of surgery, called "Welfare Applications" when prisoners would tell me their worries, ask me to write letters for them, or make contacts at home. These men were often skilled in manipulation, and made an art form of beating the world's systems. Some were brilliant artists. One copied a lovely painting he had admired on my office wall (with permission). Another drew cartoons for prisoners to send home, doubtless conning the family that this was his own work. Another had forged American dollars, and UK MOT certificates as a sideline. The challenge was to persuade some that there were ways of using that talent outside which would still bring in money and not endanger their liberty. For most that was a forlorn hope. Just occasionally there were sparks of enlightenment. Still, the debates between us were fun and I got along with some real rogues. I had to develop an understanding with each individual that I dealt in truth. My job was focussed on their future in the real world with real families and real temptations. By implication – I hoped they could change – but in the meantime sometimes they shared some of their hopes and fears. When one London Bank Robber, doing 10 years, told me he was worried about his son who had been sent to Borstal, I gently got him to admit that he had not been the best of role models. This was a skill which was God-given to most Probation Officers. No one actually taught me the words to say, but training in Listening Skills helped me to LISTEN first, show empathy, and then give feedback by indirect reflective comments rather than direct questions. My future students would recognise this as a theme tune based on the teachings of Carl Rogers, but it was not until 1982 that I read Rogerian theory, as far as I can recollect. [45] I remember one man telling me that every time he went out of prison (some 15 times before – his record told me) he would "go to Woollies to buy a torch and a pair of gloves". "How about just considering that NEXT TIME, yes that will come, one day, you might try a different…" "Different shop?" he said. I dared to say that his record did not look like he was a very successful burglar. He did not thump me! We had a laugh together. I thank God that I learnt how to be serious, and how to get alongside these really deeply wounded men, and began to pray that I would always know when to move forward, and when to hold back.

In later years I read the excellent Christian books of David Augsburger – "Caring enough to confront" and "Caring enough to forgive…or not forgive". [46] I had much practical experience in prison, and with hindsight I wish I had read those books earlier. I wish I had more space to recall some of the many characters I met in Parkhurst. So much is confidential and unrepeatable. I used to spend the half hour on the ferry with a cup of tea and my diary, planning the day and recalling important things to remember. Names and family details were important, and using them showed that you really wanted to make a link. I arrived in the prison at 8am, so I could greet many of them as they prepared to go to work. Some wanted to show me the latest letter from their girlfriend, or the model ship they made in their cell last night. "Home visits" to their cells were always revealing. What they put on their walls told the (prison) world what they wanted you to know, but absence of female nudes also told me a lot too. Every day I saw a "lifer" whose cell was opposite my office/cell. He boasted that his story was featured in Tony Parker's book on sex offenders – "The Twisting Lane". [47] I was sorry that his exploits gave him "Kudos" among male prisoners (He had assaulted many women) whereas, if he had assaulted children he would have had to seek "Rule 43" protection[48]. [48] This bit of male mentality defeats my understanding. I never ceased to be horrified by sexual abuse, although I had found a lot of empathy for the immature actions of indecent exposers! (Don't worry, Mary. I am not about to become a "streaker" at Wembley Stadium!) Just another couple of true stories to give a bit of the flavour of this job, which had so many facets and learning opportunities.

"Doing bird" [49]

Prisoners were allowed to keep one budgie in a cage – but never to let it fly free – except one! This bird flew round, landed on your shoulder, and told you your fortune in a wonderful command of swear-words. Officers and prisoners alike loved it! One day an officer accidentally trod on the budgie. Horrified, he scooped it up and quickly got it to the vet in Cowes, and fortunately it was mended. Later the bird became an escapee. It managed to get out of the cell window and disappeared. A message went out on local Radio and press "Lost one budgie. Will be known by its fowl language" Sure enough the bird had fancied a seaside holiday, and was found by a surprised person who fortunately recognised the bird by its wide vocabulary. It was soon back "inside". It brought a whole new meaning to the English slang description of a prison sentence, "Doing your bird".

20. A homeless wanderer

"A serious offender whom nobody loved"

Robert was one of many lonely, homeless, and in his case, friendless creatures. Robert was doing 10 years for arson. He had tried to start a small fire to demonstrate his annoyance with a manger in his factory – then found it got out of hand.When I saw his record I knew that it was "out of his league". There he was in the same prison as men known by their "News of the World" stories. However, We learnt to read beyond the headlines. Robert's record showed that he had appeared in some 20 courts around the British Isles – often for stealing a bicycle to get from A to B. This man had a tragic history. His wife and children had been killed in a motor accident and he had just roamed the country aimlessly scratching or cadging a living. I got to know Robert well because he had the knack of making everyone dislike him by pestering you with personal comments. Hence he had spent every one of his numerous short sentences in a single cell. All of his relatives had rejected him. I was determined that during this sentence I would try to help him understand how he was such an expert in upsetting people – by not letting him upset me. He was still at Parkhurst when I left, but I decided to write to him as an outside Probation Officer. He called me "Uncle Dave". I never gave my home address to any prisoner, but made "an exception with Robert. He never took advantage of that. Once I forgot to write to him for a month, and he had lost my address. One day a policeman knocked at my door asking "Excuse me, but are you Uncle Dave? There's this prisoner who wonders whether you are dead because he hasn't heard from you." When he got to the end of his sentence he was released to Rampton Secure Hospital because his odd behaviour made psychiatrists feel he was a danger to the Community, and possibly to himself. I visited him at Rampton, and liaised with social workers there about his discharge plans. They found him a flat in a tall block in a new area in northern England. We had sought to encourage his positive hobby of making dolls houses to unusual designs (manor houses with swimming pools) and he wanted to donate these to children's ward of hospitals. The social workers who settled him in his new home built on this skill – and Robert developed a reputation for these unusual dolls houses. There was an article in the local newspaper about them. It did not mention prison. He had somehow made a new life. The police knew him well. He drank a lot of coffee and did not sleep well. They found him wandering at night, lonely but not doing anyone any harm. He had been befriended by the local library and a café where he spent a lot of time. This lonely man was helped by his new community – who learnt to ignore his eccentricities and give him what he needed – friendship and acceptance. Mary and I visited him in his ninth floor apartment. He treated us like Royalty. On his walls were many completed jigsaws mounted and hung as his pictures. He sat us down to a feast of fish (fingers) and peas, and mashed potato. He waited on us with white towel over his arm. Around him were partly finished dolls houses. I had been convinced that he was a very hurt man who in the end would never intentionally hurt another person. Local people gave him a chance – and he did not let them – or me down. When he died I found he had nominated me as his next of kin. There were only five of us at his funeral. He was buried in a paupers' grave, It was the deepest I had ever seen. He had never accepted my Christianity, but I was grateful to be there and to thank God that he had spent the last six years of his life crime-free, and giving pleasure to little children through his dolls houses. The Librarian was also a minister, and he conducted the funeral. Robert gave me an atlas which was quite symbolic of the wandering soul who now found rest.

"Through-care"

"After-Care" became "Through-Care" over the years as the emphasis of our job changed. I always felt that we had moved on from Police Court Missionaries, but we did try to treat "offenders" as individuals - as the story of Robert may tell you.

21 Prison Pressures and Opportunities

Prisons contain many rogues, but also many sad people who are rejected and sometimes embittered. Some are dangerous, even in custody, and manipulative, scheming to use you to beat the system.. My time there was before the days of the film "Porridge" – but I met many of those characters daily. It was good having good colleagues and we learnt a lot from each other. In fact Adrian was only my boss for half of my time in Parkhurst, but during that year we did some innovatory work as a team. He deserved much credit, as he was the first "Senior Probation Officer" in Parkhurst, and just after he started working there serious rioting broke out (nothing to do with him I hasten to add). A new Governor was appointed and many new ways of working were designed. I felt very privileged to be a member of his Probation Team at such a time of positive change, after traumatic events when spilt blood underlined just how important it was to get all methods improved. I found myself in a team seeking to re-think their roles and methods of working. For example, we were the first long term prison (other than Grendon Underwood, the Psychiatric Prison) to hold regular pre-release groups to prepare prisoners for discharge. Few of us had had any specific Group Work Training – so we had to work out our methods together. Often we had three of these new groups going every week. We read up much theory, and had a Group Leaders' Support Group to help us to learn by sharing experiences. Basically we were trying to help prisoners who were at the end of a long sentence to face the sort of issues they would face when going back to their home area, or making a fresh start somewhere else. Often they could apply for a trial weekend leave just prior to release The Group Leaders would usually support their application for this privilege, and the group would help each prisoner think of the possible pleasures, temptations, and problems ahead. Then, when the weekend had come we wondered whether the person would have the courage to come back. (It took courage to knock on the prison door to be let in!) Surprisingly, most of them did return. They then reported back to the group how it had gone – as much as they wanted to share. Of course the other men wanted to know the juicier bits. At least it made others think "What will happen when I go next month?" If prisoners did not come back we could then talk about the temptations to re-offend, or get sucked back into the gangs, drink or drugs – or domestic conflict. Some thought about such issues with a degree of realism for the first time. Some would seek a private chat with me to sort out issues they could not tell the group. For prisoners with longer sentences there were also possibilities of easing out gently by applying to go to a hostel in London to work outside each weekday, returning for custody at night. So during the last six months the prisoner was having a taste of being trusted to work in the community, prob-ably for the first time for 6 or even 10 years. Again we would try to help them prepare for this. Each group had to have a staff member (Prison or Probation Officer) sitting in on every ses-sion (for security reasons) During an Alcoholics Anonymous Group, the leader would normally be a recovered alcoholic from outside the prison. These groups were often quite awesome as they often worked to the Twelve Steps principles of AA. People attending needed to express their desire to change. Each one would have the opportunity to tell their life story – and why they wanted to change. I will always remember one black man who was doing two life sentences for killing two girlfriends when drunk. Repeatedly I heard him express his regret and wish that he could change. I believed him to be sincere and desperately sorry that he could not put the clock back. He may never be given the chance to try again. It did help them all to express their powerlessness over alcohol, and their need of a Higher Power as they understood him. It was awesome to hear them end each meeting with the Serenity Prayer. [50.] Together they asked their "Higher Power" to help them "accept the things we cannot change, to give the courage to change the things we can and to them the wisdom to learn the difference".

A bigger test for me came when 16 of the 24 prisoners on the wing where I worked asked to have an AA group of their own. They were on "Rule 43", segregated for their protection because of the nature of their offences, mainly sexual abuse. This raised other issues, but they also may well be released one day. If alcohol was a factor which was major to their offending pattern it was considered that they might benefit from an AA Group too. The Governor's Meeting agreed that we could conduct an experiment with this, and, because I had been the staff member on another Alcoholics Anonymous Group I was asked to be part of this group. It was for me a priviedged experience for me, as I learnt how alcohol had contributed to their offending from their own testimony. The AA member who came in to facilitate the group was consistently magnificent in not allowing them to project their guilt onto drink. He stressed that they all could CHOOSE to beat the alcohol, and the addiction to sex. He stressed his view that the same principles applied to all addictions. That group made me think hard about a lot of things. Within a few years the Alpha Drug Rehabilitation Centre in Hampshire, near to where I subsequently worked, opened a sister centre to conduct a Home Office-funded experiment based on the principle which that group leader had put forward that persistent re-offending demonstrated symptoms similar to addiction and could be [51] treated using the same Behaviourist principles which they used to treat drug addiction. The time in Parkhurst taught me a great deal about "Prison Pressures". Although they were often harder to find, there were also real opportunities. I do believe that by setting limited and realistic aims, we did some imaginative work. We never had ways of measuring it, but we were convinced that we had some impact on some prisoners and their families. We at least increased the possibility that some might try to find the motivation and the means to change. Realistically, with many long term prisoners it was against great odds. That was because some were addicted "recidivists", but at least with "through-care", parole and contacts with hostels and family home (when one still existed) we felt we were travelling hopefully with some people. With experience these guarded aims became more achievable. Unusually, Adrian Stanley and I were both members British Association of Social Workers' Treatment of Offenders' Committee. Adrian chaired that national committee for two years and we held two national conferences for over 200 people on Serious Young Offenders, and Mentally Abnormal Offenders. (We were also in the Probation Officers' Union, NAPO and worked with them in these conferences). In 1978 we had a unique opportunity to present "Evidence to the House of Commons Expenditure Committee on Prison Pressures." [52] At a time when there were many questions about such things as unrest, riots and Overcrowding. "Was any positive work done in Prison towards rehabilitation or treatment?" We had lots of views on all of that and it was wonderful to have a public platform for our direct observations, based on a reasoned argument and our written evidence. Four of us were examined for over an hour in those magnificent surroundings. It has been fascinating to see again our words in print (in Hansard) 32 years on, and the comments of members of Parliament. We concentrated on our positive belief, based on day-to-day experience that Social Workers' contributions could and did make in Prison, through-care, and especially the work which Adrian had done with mentally abnormal offenders on the "mini Broadmoor" in Parkhurst. Additionally I was asked questions about my experience on a one- week placement with the Probation services in Columbus Ohio with Projects which diverted offenders from custody – or even court proceedings. (I had spent a week with the Ohio State Probation Service, and visited Diversion projects there, gathering information for BASW en route. Everywhere the Americans put down the red carpet and the Deputy Chief Probation Officer took me everywhere with him – including three large prisons and many courts.) It was good to discuss issues of Care and Control, and our concerns to challenge offenders to try to change behaviour – if they were capable of it. [53] Through BASW and NAPO we sought to gain information and stimulate debate about pressures within the Prison, Probation and Social Work services.

Adrian had powerful articles published in the "Justice of Peace" and "Prison Services Journal" and contributed to what has become a 1968 "classic" on "Authority in Social Casework" by Foren and Bailey.[54 & 55]

When we both retired early from the Probation Service (1989) we still campaigned to reduce the number of prisoners in custody (about 40,000). The overflow from prison were being held in local police station cells. The number of prisoners has since [56] doubled in 20 years. Nevertheless, Probation Officers have valiantly pursued the provision of realistic alternatives to custody – as well as social work through-care initiatives.

22. "Pride comes before a fall"

A true cautionary tale.

More benefits of hindsight? On 19th June 1980 Adrian Stanley chaired a Plenary Session of the Conference on Mentally Abnormal Offenders. He was well qualified as he specialised in working with some of the nation's most notorious criminals. The list of speakers was like a "Who's Who" of Criminologists and Practitioners in Probation and Penal institutions. We took great pride in having assembled an illustrious group of speakers from the mental health, prison, social work and legal professions. My former Home Office tutor, Herschel Prins, was the keynote speaker. However, I had reviewed his very knowledgeable book in "Social Work Today" – and I was quite pleased by what I had written. However, I had dared to criticise such an eminent man in print. I made a big point in the review that I had been amazed that he, a trainer of Social Workers, had devoted so few paragraphs to "Social Work in Prison". Suddenly, here I was (horror of horrors) face-to-face with the author, today's Keynote Speaker, the one to whom I owe so much and I had dared "rubbish his book"!! As I walked into the Malvern Abbey Hotel lecture hall, Herschel Prins greeted me –

"I hear you have been kind enough to review my book".
"He can't have read the review" I thought!

Adrian quietly chuckled. Herschel Prins greeted me with a warm handshake – but it was me who was shaking! In a flash I doubted my competence. "What had I written?" (I had worked hard at it and read other books to check out what I was saying but *what right had I got to be critical of* <u>him</u>??) How my pride got pricked. He just walked on to next business (His lecture). Somehow I managed my job on a Panel, but I went straight back later to my hotel room to check what I had written. Actually I had been greatly impressed by everything in the book. The Title alone (" Offenders, Deviants, or Patients?") spoke out what we in Parkhurst often found ourselves thinking. We had always commented that you could take 100 of our "prisoners" and change them with 100 of Broadmoor's "patients" and nobody would know the difference. The constant issue was to find ways of helping and de-labelling them when and if they are ready to be discharged into the real world – which was that Conference majored on. It was a privilege to be among that group of experts who cared about many whom Society would discard as "dangerous lunatics" – or worse. The memory of that shock came back to my mind several times in future years – and like other such memories it got magnified. Telling myself not to be so silly, I decided to do what I would recommend to others. ***"Pray about it and send an apology."***

So it was 30 years later that I looked Herschel Prins up on the Internet and e-mailed him. I began by underlining my gratitude for his tuition and offered my apologies for that review. He replied in generous tones, saying he had since written some ten other books – and he had felt "the review was perfectly reasonable." He was on the third edition of the book! His letter ended –

"Very best wishes – and for times past,
Sincerely, Herschel P."

Time and again I have found that facing worries head on always clears the air.

23. Discharged from Prison – what next?

The Hampshire Probation bosses had been thinking – and they did have some discharge plans for me. "If he was to build on some six years' Probation experience he could do with some more training." I was enthusiastic to learn more skills – but although promotion might follow, I never wanted to leave the "hands on" job. They "hedged their bets" and sent me to London on the National Institute for Social Work's "One Year Course in Further Social Work Studies". This meant being away from home all week for a year. Another sacrifice for Mary.

Certainly Hampshire Probation sent me to London for the One Year Course in management, training, group work, and community work at the National Institute for Social Work Training. The plan was that this would equip me to be a trainer. I enjoyed three days each week learning in groups and lectures, and on the other two days I was attached to the training team of Buckinghamshire Social Services Department. It was amazing experience to be part of this team, and to supervise one student in Residential Child Care.

The theoretical and practical training about Group work was very useful for my future Careers, and it emphasised how we could have used this information well when experimenting with small groups in Parkhurst. The intensive instruction in "Training and Supervision" was given by some of the country's leading social work experts and for the rest of my careers I was always indebted to them for excellent foundations. When the course was over, I applied for the role of Trainer of Probation Students in Hampshire. This should have been almost a formality, as they had sponsored me on the course, but I made a "real hash" of the interview (The Chief Probation Officer's words – or something like them!) Nevertheless, I believe that what they eventually appointed me to was even better.

24 Community Development : **WORKING TOGETHER**

I became the Senior Probation Officer on one of the largest Council Housing Estates in the country, Leigh Park, in Havant.

81

Two years later I was enabled to have an article published in "Social Work Today" [57]. I entitled the article "Community Development and Crime" and this caused something of a stir locally because it told a lot of "home truths" about this estate which in my opinion had been unfairly labelled. In 24 years the population of Havant had trebled by 34, 000 people being moved out of Portsmouth 8 miles away. The facilities did not always keep pace with the movement of people. There was a comparatively high crime rate, but the residents wanted to settle into a more "leafy" environment from quite a poor area of the city. The day after the article was published nationally I received a phone call from a local dignitary. "So you're the person who wants to set up a Volunteer Bureau when we've already got one?!" I replied "Thank you for telling me that can we get to know each other ? Perhaps you would like to come to the Social Worker's Luncheon Club next week?" He came, and we got on well, eventually. The National Institute Course had taught us to work closely together with all agencies, to tackle Community Issues. A social workers' luncheon club helped us to find allies, and to look objectively at this Community. We had vowed early on to

"Never do separately anything we could do better together."

18 Years of

OFF THE RECORD

1977 - 1995

A Counselling and Information Service for Young People

The estate of new houses had 35% of Havant's population, but 54% of the children of single parents and overcrowded households. Professional and Voluntary agencies worked together to set up play and nursery facilities and Southampton University sponsored a "New Communities Project". This set up "Focus 230" – a Community Work-base. We help set up a battered wives refuge. A wonderful magistrate called "Betty Bell", who was a local resident and campaigner for the underprivileged, was a great inspiration and supporter of all new initiatives. The Education, Youth, Social Services and Probation together set up a Working Group to start a Teenagers' Phone-in Information and Counselling Service. I chaired this Working Party and helped train the volunteers. We looked at models in Hammersmith, Bristol and similar estates. So *"Off the Record"* was born, like one of the same name in Bristol. Bristol OTR let us use their training and promotion ideas – and a local trainer gave his time to the team. It was exciting, as we publicised it. After training some 30 volunteers, no one phoned for the first month!!! But then the calls rolled in and young people began to value the new service. It was based in the Methodist Church in the centre of the Estate, on "neutral territory". (There was already some gang formation). elected and trained. The volunteers were great soon learnt to be excellent "*listeners*" rather that advisors. (For me it was wonderful preparation for setting up a counselling service for adults, and training volunteers for it, over 20 years later!) Need I say it? **God's timing is always right.**

When I left Havant(with a lot of sadness, after 7 exciting years, "Off the Record" moved to another central Community resource called Point Seven. (Where Probation volunteers had run a group for Prisoners' wives and children.) This base was expanded and provided a 24 bedded hostel for homeless young people. This was the Community response to the fact that the biggest problem presented by youth on that estate was homelessness – and unemployment. I was privileged to return for the opening ceremony - by the comedian, Lenny Henry. The 18th Birthday celebrations were salutary for me – but I was glad it happened..! When I walked quietly into a packed hall no one recognised me for 20 minutes! I sat and quietly read the information leaflets on the chairs, Then someone said "Hello!" They had moved on well – and provided still a great community resource and had an Off the Record off-shoot in Portsmouth! **They had done well – without me.! For a moment that came as a shock. Then the truth dawned on me.** *I had to "let go and let God"* **. This new service had come of age, and was really serving the young people of that needy community. Togetherness had paid off! Praise the Lord!** In 2011 I was sent a copy of the **Portsmouth News** in which it was reported that "Off the Record" had just been awarded the **Queen's Award for Service to the Community. I congratulate them for developing the work we started over 30 years ago. It is an excellent example of voluntary and statutory agencies working together imaginatively.**

I really loved working in Havant – especially on that needy estate. As Senior Probation Officer I had attended dozens of Case Conferences on Child Abuse, and learned to trust fellow professionals and to handle confidential personal dynamite. We had innovatory group-work with young offenders, a car mainte-nance group for young car thieves, and a sailing boat for local adventure and for delinquents to enjoy law- abiding fun. We had specialist "Through and after Care" with serious offenders and their families. We had fun on the way – and also picked up many broken relationships. They were wonderful colleagues and friends, **for a season.**

But the work which left its deepest memory was working with conflicts and poverty and reconciliation work in *families* and the ***youth counselling with volunteers*** who just wanted to give time and talents to listen to and help disadvantaged people. I thank God for those seven years. It was my colleagues from Probation and other agencies who worked so well together - purposively. Volunteers came from all churches and none; teachers, youth workers, community workers, play scheme workers, volunteers who gave friendship to prisoners' families. With shared aims, it was done ***TOGETHER.***

25. "Letting go and letting God"

After seven good years in Havant, with Teresa having successful got good "A Levels" she started training to be a teacher in Bath, I was once again convinced that we should face changes. We decided that I should seek different Probation work near Gloucestershire where Adrian Stanley had become Senior Probation Officer in Cheltenham. I applied to manage "Barbican" Probation Day Centre in Gloucester. This had a good national reputation as a centre for homeless and unemployed people – with a multi-talented staff of group workers and educationalists.

A preliminary visit told me that it represented a real challenge, but would enable me to gain more experience – whilst still keeping a "hands-on" job working with needy people. My observation was that the centre needed some serious changes if it was to help the Gloucestershire Probation Service to meet its aims. Although it was helping many needy people less than half of its clientele were offenders. At the interview I proposed that the Centre change to be a real "Alternative to custody". With the Gloucester Prison across the road, it had shouted to me that we should major on giving people more realistic alternatives in life to crime and prison sentences.

The law was about to change to allow "Conditions" to be added to Probation Orders so that, instead of imposing a prison sentence, a Court could substitute a Probation Order with a 60 day Condition to attend a Day Centre, with a structured programme of education, social skills, and groups designed to help people face their problems (such as addictions or illiteracy). I argued that my group-work and community-work experience did equip me for that job. This was what the interviewing committee was waiting to hear, so I was appointed. Little did I realise just how great was the task. It was hard for some of the staff team to accept the degree of change that was needed. Here was a centre which people visited from all over the country, and rightly commended the work. Unusual for a Probation Day Centre they had a Play group, mainly to help single parent mothers and children. They taught parenting skills. Homeless men came daily for a "shower and a shave – and tea and a chat." A wood-working workshop enabled men to make such things as "Wendy houses" out of scrap wood. They provided an alcohol-free environment, They provided lunches at weekends for homeless people and gave advice to poor people on money management. Here was I, a newcomer wanting to make changes. Even though they saw the sense in the legislation, I was not popular with my new colleagues! Slowly we made the necessary changes. Discussions in a women's social skills group revealed the need for a group to help families that had experienced domestic abuse, and this linked in with new community groups for survivors of domestic violence.

We also worked closely with the Probation Hostel for alcoholics and eventually plans for starting much more work with homeless people arose from people who had worked in both of the probation projects. All of these projects have moved on in strength over nearly 20 years – and Community Liaison has also developed from these beginnings. It was also an exciting time when Probation was involved in the development of the Victim Support schemes in Gloucestershire. Much credit must be given to Magistrates, Politicians, Social Services and Probation managers who facilitated all of these developments – including much co-operation between voluntary and statutory agencies. These were pioneer days, and I want to pay tribute to those who took risks in making changes which led to improved social work and community care provisions – often at great personal cost. Many volunteers gave many hours of talent. We have learnt to value the contributions of people of all races, faiths - and none.

After four years at the Barbican Centre I moved to be Senior Probation officer in South Gloucestershire, based in Stroud. Here I led a team of six probation Officers who each had a "patch" in a rural and a small town area. For three years I was privileged to work with more groups of talented people, both in statutory and voluntary agencies. Again we worked well **together** and saw many needy people find peace in struggles in domestic and social situations. This was the time when Victim Support Schemes were starting in most areas, and I was involved in this in Gloucestershire. It was satisfying, innovatory work, but God had one more challenge on His agenda.

There was to be *just one more 4am "Call to Change."*

I felt increasingly that somehow God wanted me to move on. I decided to "test the water" by doing a one year evening course in my spare time at one of the pioneer Christian Counselling Services in Britain – Network Counselling Services, Bristol. Here I was immensely privileged to "sit at the feet"of Roger Hurding. Roger has a great knowledge of both secular and Christian schools of counselling and psychotherapeutic services. He had also struggled with much ill-health (including blindness) and found great healing and inner strength.[58] I could not have had a better bridge-building exercise. The team at Network was extremely talented and knowledgeable. We were led through Gary Collins' book, Duncan Buchanan's "The Counselling of Jesus", and across the whole library of Counselling of which Roger Hurding seemed to have an intimate grasp. I found some examples of books with which I had spent days struggling; Roger's "Roots and Shoots" [59] seemed to sum each one up in a couple of pages. It was a feast which enlightened and thrilled me each week.

So when we in the Gloucestershire Probation Service were given the opportunity to apply for early retirement I was not surprised to wake at 4am one day, knowing that God was challenging me again to get out of my comfort zone. In 1987 I had trained and been Accredited as a Methodist Local Preacher, and I asked the Superintendent Minister Vernon Godden to talk and pray with me about the way forward. No one could have been better suited. Vernon had many years experience as a Prison Chaplain, and was Chairman of the Trustees of the Langley House Trust – which provided homes and rehabilitation for prisoners. He knew what I was leaving behind – and to what God was now calling me. I just said that I believed that God was calling me to test out whether there was a need for a Christian Counselling Service like Network in Gloucestershire – and if so, I would need some kind of work to top up my Probation pension should I decide to retire. I also needed the vital exercise of discussing this all with Mary, who would once again have to face changes – and a reduced income! She bravely agreed – as long as it did not entail moving again. Shortly afterwards Vernon offered me a part-time job as a Lay Worker with the Methodist Church in Gloucester Circuit. It seemed strange making a case out to Gloucestershire Probation Service for them to allow me to retire after 22 years' service in a job I loved. Nevertheless, I put forward financial and other arguments which persuaded them to grant it. So four months later I started four years of excellent experience. Working under Vernon was a privilege. He had the knack of throwing me in the deep end of any Pastoral work which came along. Vernon got me involved in the healing ministry, and for the first time I did bereavement counselling and officiated at funerals.

I was extremely glad of this "Baptism of Fire" (to mix the metaphors). Vernon was a great role model and taught me much about the importance of prayer. It was during this period that I was introduced to Selwyn Hughes' "Everyday with Jesus" Bible readings, and these remain my daily sustenance 30 years later. Like many others of the millions of readers, I found that each day's lesson seemed to be just for me- or someone I was helping.

Then I had another 3 years in another church involved in youth club, elderly persons day centres, and much pastoral work. Not having had any experience of hospital visiting this proved invaluable preparation for what lay ahead. My friend, Adrian Stanley, was also granted early retirement, and he soon found employment as Assistant General Secretary with the Langley House Trust. [29]Adrian soon had me doing some part time work with Langley House, leading some 20 short courses in Listening Skills for their staff. There were amazing "God-incidences" also, as in Gloucester Royal Hospital I met one Julia Conway (Head of the School of Midwifery and former missionary to the Zulus) and in the Langley House Trust at Cheltenham I met one Sarah Jones who had MA in Counselling and Psychotherapy.

It is the essence of my story that along His Way that God gave me wonderful travelling companions. Julia and Sarah were God-given trainers who would be essential for any Counselling Service., Maureen Godden was a lovely Administrator. So much talent was already waiting in the

wings, all known to God but until then unknown to me. So that leads on to Part Three.

"Towards a Christian Counselling Service for Gloucestershire"

Part Three

Towards a Christian Counselling Service

26. Making Preparations

It was an exciting time. Things were coming together. I had met Rev Charles Garrett, a Gloucestershire Baptist Minister who had also completed a Network Course, and was planning to set up a small group at Wotton-under-Edge. We had both admired the pioneers who had set up Network and eventually we shared a vision for a similar service in Gloucestershire. I particularly valued the whole Training Team at Network, and the support systems which they had in place. The imaginative way in which this Christian Counselling Service had developed, especially as it had been one of the first in the UK. It seemed such a good model. I became determined that we should do our best to allow this to spread into Gloucester. The enthusiasm of the team was infectious. The hush of anticipation for each training evening was strangely heightened by their belief that Roger Hurding would reveal new truths discovered from his depth and breadth of knowledge. Roger never disappointed. As I read his "Roots and Shoots" and "Restoring the Image" [55] I marvelled at the ways I could link up my training from the Home Office, Tavistock Clinic or Probation with what Roger was presenting. What he did in particular specially was to show God's hand at work in the healing that he described. He weaved psychology, listening skills, and theology together into a wholeness that I had previously only glimpsed. Week after week I became enthralled and convinced that I must be part of this God-inspired profession. I went home bubbling with praise to our Creator who was continually enthusing me with new visions. That feeling of wonderment never left me, and it drove me to seek more revelations. "What next?" Thus, when I was successful in applying for early retirement from Probation I knew that somehow God would prepare the way for me to be part of His Plan for another "Network-type" service in Gloucester. It seemed as if, step by step, God was planning experiences which enabled me to grow through filling in gaps in my knowledge. For example, bereavement counselling, hospital visiting and the healing and prayer ministry were vital dimensions I had not yet studied nor participated in.

The time I spent working as a Lay Worker allowed important contacts to be made. Vernon Godden enabled me to meet many from other churches, and the ecumenical links were invaluable. It was most challenging to find myself suddenly put in charge of contacting all the people who were willing to visit in Gloucester and Cheltenham for the Billy Graham campaign called "Mission 89". This was quite onerous for me as a "new boy on the block" – but as it was Vernon who was commending me to them, I was well accepted by the many church leaders I was privileged to meet. Vernon kept "throwing me in at the deep end" and somehow God enabled me to keep afloat!

I was enabled to officiate at four funerals, which was new territory. This included the funeral of a 7 year old boy, whose family were referred to us by the hospital. Each of these stretched me differently - but Vernon assured me that God never gives you a job without supplying the equipment to do it, and that proved amazingly right.

On more familiar ground, we started a club for over 40 young people at the second Church where we ministered together, (Lonsdale Road), and I enjoyed working at a day facility for the elderly, and a Bible study for mothers from a playgroup. This was a wonderful all-age apprenticeship whilst preparing to start the Counselling Service which was emerging simultaneously.

In Hucclecote Methodist Church, Gloucester, I was enabled to be part of the Prayer and Healing Team, with monthly healing services, and then to that become part of the Gloucester Royal Hospital Ministry Team. All of this was new and invaluable as it put me in touch with Christians from all strands of "churchmanship". The hospital Chaplain's imaginative ecumenical team started weekly "Services of Prayer for the sick with laying on of hands", and sought out Christians on the hospital staff. This presented many wonderful opportunities to speak and pray with many needy people, and to share ministry with people from other denominations. Little did I know that one of this team would eventually share my vision for a Christian Counselling Service! A former Baptist Missionary, Julia Conway, the Head of the School of Midwifery also caught the vision for "the birth of this new service." Here was a proven trainer, who was supportive from the outset. Is it any surprise that our first two training courses were born in Schools of Midwifery? "God was on the case!"

27. Testing the waters" and being tested[56]

Discussions with **Maureen and Vernon Godden** and others confirmed that God wanted us to "test the waters". John Turner of Network and a founding member of Network's Council of Management agreed to join our "Council of Reference". He first helped us tell the Christians of Gloucester the story of Bristol's Network of caring Christians whose faith was worked out through the service of Counselling. I wrote, therefore, to every Church Leader in Gloucester, inviting them to send representatives to a meeting entitled **"Towards a Christian Counselling Service for Gloucester"**. The letters went out. We waited for the response. We prayed! What a response! I could not believe it when NINETY PEOPLE came!!! I knew some of them, and was pleased that there was a good inter-denominational spread. Thankfully, there were many we did not know - but the word had gone out and the room buzzed with enthusiasm. Several local people talked of the need for Christian Counselling in Gloucester, and then John Turner of Network told of their experience in Bristol. They had depended so much on voluntary gifts of time and talents and money, as well as an excellent training team and course. They outlined how there were several services like Network emerging across the nation, and meeting real needs. People soon realised that we were pioneers in a new developing Christian ministry. The Network Group gave a very good description of their progress and advised us to set up an interdenominational Working Group. They assured us that if enough people were convinced that the vision was right, the ones whom God had chosen would come forward. Most importantly, Network offered their advice and guidance along the way. I expressed my appreciation of all they had given to me personally through the Training Course. (They even eventually allowed me to develop our initial training based on their material! And guided me through it.) Before the end of that eventful evening more than 15 people had offered help – and the first meeting of the Working Group was arranged. In the meantime people were asked to pray about inviting along others who might be helpful I asked that people did not "hide their lights under a bushel" but let me know what gifts of knowledge or life experience which they or others had which could be helpful. In the end this process just confirmed God's provision. During the next few weeks people's shyness quickly wore off as several Church Leaders, and people with teaching, nursing, counselling, social work, youth work, and administration experience offered help. Some people said they were able to find others who could some of the necessary gifts to offer.

Someone recommended that I approach Rev David Bick. He was a respected Anglican Minister, a Clinical Theologian, who had written and taught about prayer ministry, group-work, and "Wholeness through Christ". David Bick lived in the grounds of Prinknash Abbey. I determined to contact him immediately.

So we went away from that remarkable meeting eagerly anticipating the first meeting of the Working Group, each one doubtless reflecting on their role in this new venture. The advice to contact David Bick proved inspired wisdom. I was quickly convinced that he would become a good mentor. He and I met frequently over the next eleven years. He brought a whole new range of dimensions to my thinking – notably through his intimate knowledge of the teachings of Frank Lake.[57] the multi-facetted chain of Christians from the spectrum of God's Rainbow Kingdom. "Together" seemed to be the theme of our way. David Bick was an important link in forward, and along the way God seemed to be providing so many people who had sampled God's Healing Love, who rested on His Word, who found His guidance their Rock. I needed this staying power and reflection and mentoring guidance so often.

I cannot emphasize too much that God gave me travelling companions at every turn who revealed contrasting life stories and different dimensions of God's Wisdom. This was and is His Way. My frequent prayer was given me by David Bick –

"Teach me Your Way, O Lord,
   Help me to walk in your Truth,
   Give me an undivided heart
   That I may fear your Name."[58]

This remains my oft-repeated lighthouse. Roger Hurding showed frequently the relevance of Scripture to all human behaviour. During one trip to America I devoured Gary Collins' book "Christian Counselling" over three weeks and related every scriptural quotation to the situation or problem he was describing". It was a most exciting exercise. [59] Similarly David Bick wrote about "The use of the Psalms for spiritual and emotional growth"[60] and in the latter part of this book you will learn of one remarkable healing where a client of mine was healed principally because of a Psalm which David Bick gave to him in an inspired way.

"Together" being put to the test.

So we eagerly waited for the first meeting of the Working Group – a group of some 16 Christians, many of whom recognised and greeted each other. As we waited, three men in black clerical suits came to join us. They entered enquiringly with an air of authority (almost accusingly) and glanced round the room – seeking out people they knew. They spotted leaders of evangelical churches. They looked at me *"Where are the Catholics?"* My heart fell! (So far we had none!) From across the room a small voice whispered ..... *"but Catholics aren't Christians*! "* My heart crashed! I breathed an arrowed prayer heavenwards *"We cannot begin like that – PLEASE" "Can we just pause for a quiet Prayer?"* After a brief silence, I thanked God for bringing us TOGETHER, for His Purposes, to do His Will. "Help us Lord to seek Your will at all times, and put our differences aside, as we celebrate how you made us all individuals. You LOVE us all and called each of us here today to seek the Way forward - in Love and fellowship...." Those were not my exact words of course (I seldom write prayers, but in emergencies I do believe that God gives us the words to say! And he certainly hears our petitions from the heart and that was from mine!) Some of us had prayed beforehand about that meeting. Now was not the time to have the meeting destroyed! Now was the time to come TOGETHER! And we DID.... Just!

28. The Way Forward

After that we introduced ourselves and discussed how best to proceed. I had produced a draft list of some important issues which we needed to address and we added to this by "brainstorming". I requested for us all "Teach me YOUR WAY O Lord" He answered that prayer continually. God seemed to be saying to me that in future I needed to take a step back and choose someone else who would propose one of those men in clerical suits to chair future meetings – to guide us forward in seeking His Will.

*"No temptation has seized you except what is common to man. And God is faithful; he will not let you be tempted beyond what you can bear. But when you are tempted **he will also provide you with a way out** so that you can stand up under it.* [61]

(I wish I had known this verse when I worked in Parkhurst Prison . Even though I know the "Word of God is sharper than a two edged sword" (Hebrews 4:12), it would have been no good using it as a blunt instrument it to impress prisoners. Roger Hurding taught me that too!) The Holy Spirit did provide much more than "a way out". This new Chairman of our meetings enabled us to move forward and prioritise. At the same time it freed me up to be creative in the background, which enabled others to emerge and find their places in the new organisation. We could test out Network's structure and staffing and gently develop them in our setting The structure of the Service was very important. At the point of need, people seeking help required helpers alongside them whom they could trust as "Competent to counsel" [62]

So we decided to follow Network's pattern with regard to

1. Status. To seek to become a Company Limited by Guarantee. and to apply for Charitable Status. For which we needed to design the necessary documents and complete Application forms.
2. Appointments. This required us to appoint Directors.
3. An Administrator. We were really indebted to the clear brain of Maureen Godden, who kept us in order; and other office staff who joined us later, like Miriam Morey and Jane Wood who had key roles in ensuring that new systems of record-keeping and communications were established and functioned smoothly. Vital for us all was to share an early morning prayer time.
4. A Treasurer, to procure some funds (eg from donations from supporting Churches and Individual "Members" and fees from Training Courses.) as well as design systems of accounting, etc. I was grateful to these conscientious people who kept what I called "beady eyes" on the all too small finances initially.
5. To acquire and Office and Counselling rooms which were central and accessible
6. to equip these with furniture, stationary, phones etc.
7. To recruit and train Reception staff and design rotas.
8. To design Office Procedures, Publicity material etc.

This was just the start of the long list of things which had to be done, but it demanded a whole new lot of skills from most of us, and a clear mind for the Chairman, **David Watkins,** who kept us together, pointing in the same direction. The lesson was that when we became "Purpose-driven" and single-minded we achieved everything necessary. Help came from many Christians. Some found furniture, another (Gloucester City's Chief City Valuer – **David Hook,** who just

"happened to be a friend from Lonsdale Church where I worked!) found us good offices in the YMCA building at reasonable rent. People who sampled our course but did not feel able to counsel, joined as reception staff.

The informal and formal Christian networks gave publicity and interest, and as we managed to present acceptable Introductory Courses, the message got around that we really could provide a new Christian Caring resource. **So a key concept in "Together" is to be "Purpose-driven" –and back it all with prayer.** Every person who has recalled those days has commented on how this process gave empowerment which transcended denominational boundaries. We thank all Gloucestershire Christians for their prayerful under-pinning all we did with Prayer – and sacrificial giving. "Amazing Grace!"

Together, building foundations.

Our Statement of Aims included
a. to provide an organisation which will facilitate the development of Christian Counselling within Gloucester; and to that end
b. to provide training for people who are offering themselves to become Christian Counsellors, and who are supported by their churches in that aim." [63]

Clearly the training and selection of suitable Counsellors must be the first priority. Additionally, for anyone to make referrals then it was essential to convince the public in general, and churches in particular, that a solid organisation was being set up. That is where the working Group came in, So it was important that we had respected. Church Leaders from many denominations could work together to ensure that aims were acceptable, and achievable. That much was in place – and we gave thanks to our Creator God. Suffice it to say that the Initial

Working Group oversaw all the necessary stages to get the service off the ground within a year. We designed a Statement of Aims, and applied for Charitable Status in order to become a Company Limited by Guarantee.(again following the Network pattern.) We appointed the necessary officers, including Treasurer, Administrator, Training

Team, Supervisors... We designed systems of training and operation for the Receptionists and Counsellors, and rules about record-keeping and Confidentiality. Nearly everything depended on the generous gifts from volunteers of their time and talents. Of course we realised that we would eventually have to employ a few people, and consider asking "clients" to make a contribution for their counselling in order to be able pay rent and other expenses. We were extremely grateful to have more than 70 supporting churches, and many generous individual donors. It was so important that we had so much talent in the team of volunteers who filled jobs on the Council of Management, such as being involved with publicising the service and fund-raising. It was a steep learning curve for us all, but we discovered hidden talents of all sorts. We had many people with specialised knowledge in the counselling and medical fields, who offered help, and some became a Council of Reference to whom we could go for advice when specific expertise was required. Throughout, the advice of other pioneers in Christian Counselling and Pastoral Work was invaluable. The team of Supervisors and Managers grew together, learning from each other amazingly well. Every day we thanked God for His guidance and provision and real needs were being met from the outset. There was daily confirmation that His purposes were working out.

29. Training First.

Many Christians with suitable experience emerged to become our eventual Group Facilitators and Supervisors. Julia Conway offered her School of Midwifery premises for our first course. "Amazing"! Network allowed us to use most of their Introductory Course and Initial One Year Course, which would gradually be made our own. By holding Saturday Seminars on subjects which seemed too big for a one evening session, we were able to import expertise from nearby emerging sister services. Good training was paramount. All the time we sought to improve it by seeking training for our Group Facilitators, and by importing experienced Christian Counsellors with specialist knowledge to lead whole-day seminars. (See Appendix Two)

It was an inspiring time as some 60 people booked into our first two Introductory Courses in 1990. Some 40 of those went on to complete the first One Year Course. This, coupled with the training team, proved to be the well-motivated and competent nucleus from which we could grow. On-going continuing training continued to be a vital requirement for all of us, and the first ten years saw a constant drive for us to grow in skill acquisition and to improve training methods so as to gain academic credibility nationally and locally. Suffice it to say that, in the next ten years, over 200 Christians completed the "full Course" as that changed and improved constantly. By 1995 the "full course" became a two-year, 250 hour "Foundation and Pre-Accreditation Course. This required much hard work, negotiation, testing and being tested.

COURSE IN CHRISTIAN COUNSELLING
AT
FOUNDATION
AND
ADVANCED LEVELS
PREPARATION FOR ACCREDITATION BY THE
ASSOCIATION Of CHRISTIAN COUNSELLORS

(An outline of the development of our Training Courses and Seminars from 1990-1999 is at Appendix One)

The photo of new Director Sheila Appleton with the Bishop of Tewkesbury at the opening of new offices in central Gloucester in 2005. This symbolises the ecumenical nature of Listening Post.

30. Growing in a bigger vineyard – with one "ACCord"

The Association of Christian Counsellors was founded during Listening Post's earliest days. Their leaders of "Training Standards" were paramount in guiding all new Christian services such as Listening Post. We sought to live up to ACC's motto

"To be a catalyst for excellence"

This book from now on is a story of pioneers in Christian Counselling growing and sharing, and I was thrilled to be part of that unfolding process. For me it began with Roger Hurding, and the Network Team inspiring people from Swindon, and Cardiff and Gloucester, while there were parallel stirrings in Coventry, Blackpool, Northampton, Wales and Essex. It was great for training team leaders from different services to meet and exchange news – especially on skills. This mutual support helped us all to grow.

ACC Pioneers

Dr. Mervyn Suffield,
Founding Chairperson

A rare picture of **Roger Altman**, Founder of
Barnabas Training Carmarthen, Wales.
First ACC Chair of Training, Roger published a
helpful book **"Through the Counselling Maze"**

Dr. Mike Sheldon of Royal London School of Medicine
was one of the first British trainers of Christians to
counsel. He wrote **"To bind up the broken hearted"**
published by Mission to Marriage in 1999 with Canadian,
Dave Ames.

Dave and Joyce Ames were founders of
Mission to Marriage. This new Christian
charity has helped many couples find peace in
their marriage.

ACC Pioneers

Dr, Roger Hurding's classic book on the new profession of Christian Counselling was **"Roots and Shoots"**. His **"Coping with illness", "As trees walking", and "Restoring the image"** described his own experience of God's healing. At Network Counselling in Bristol UK, Roger's remarkable gift of combining a great depth of medical and psychological theory, was interpreted and made accessible to a wide range of potential counsellors across the United Kingdom.

In the USA **Gary Collins'** complementary book **"Christian Counselling"** similarly stimulated the professional development on the other side of the Atlantic. Close links between the two associations developed.

Both writers demonstrated how again and again Biblical teaching was relevant to secular knowledge, and the Creator's healing purposes.

"Catalysts for excellence in Christian Counselling and Pastoral Care"
Training first

John and Anne Turner
Network Bristol
John was Director of Network when David
trained there and a constant supporter as
Listening Post was being formed. He was
Chair of Training Standards, ACC.

Allan and Rosemary Pavey
Barnabas, Essex
Allen Pavey was Chair of Training Standards,
ACC. We missed his "zest for life" when he
departed this earth in 2002. The obituary in
ACCord declared that his was truly "A life
well lived".

Sue Hopton and Ann Churchill,
Nottingham . Both are
multi-talented, but during the
pioneer days they majored on
Supervision Training.

Some ACC Pioneers with remarkable stories

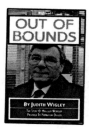

Malcolm Worsley was an habitual Criminal, having been in prison seven times. After a remarkable conversion he returned to one prison after training as a Probation Officer. Later he was the Founder of the PhilippiTrust in Blackpool, and was soon a nationally known trainer and a skilled worker with very damaged people.

Mike Fisher was Founder of The WillowsTrust in Swindon. He also works with the ACC Trauma and Abuse Group. Willows works closely in Training with Harnhill Centre for Christian Healing. Mike too is a skilled and respected Trainer in Christian Counselling.

John Nightingale was Founder of the Manna House Counselling Service in Northampton. For over 20 years he has headed up negotiations with other national and international organisations alongside David Depledge and other Chief Executives of ACC. Together these leaders of our profession have valiantly sought to be Catalysts for excellence in Christian Counselling and Care.". His wife Val has been a constant support as the Administator of Professional Standards.

Elizabeth Brazell was one of the first women to be ordained as an Anglican priest. With her husband Dennis she founded the Word for Life Trust in Hampshire, then Gloucestershire. She ran courses in Listening skills and Prayer Ministry in SE Asia and the Far East where strong missions still flourish. She was involved with the launch of Pastoral Care Membership and Training in ACC. This helped promote much needed ACC training principles and standards in pastoral work. This enthusiastic minister and carer died suddenly in 2007.
We remember her affectionately.

Many of these Pioneers could and did have life-stories or even study books written, and these will be found in the "Endnotes or Bibliography". Examples are Malcolm Worsley, Roger Altman, Selwyn Hughes, Mike Sheldon, Dave Ames.

(See Part 5 entitled "So What?) Others wrote copiously and most helpfully in the quarterly magazine, which later received the title "ACCord". It was my great privilege to enjoy fellowship with and learn from them, and many others. Each new service needed to put training first, and ACC showed us the way wonderfully well. It was a big step for ACC to extend its membership to Pastoral Workers, and Rev Elizabeth Brazell of the Word for Life Trust was the first leader of that section.

In the early days of Listening Post we had held two weekend Introductory Courses for some 80 initial Enquirers. It was a delicate business of getting to know each other's strengths, weaknesses and training needs. It was not easy to get to know, trust, assess, select and train to a sufficient minimum standard the first 30 "counsellors". These all realised that they would require further training and to have close Supervision. Fortunately our initial group of Trainers and Supervisors included some who had experience in social work or voluntary agencies . Over the next ten years our courses changed greatly, as the Training Team grew together and constantly sought to improve our service to help people who came with a wide range of problems. Our courses were Accredited by the Association of Christian Counsellors. We always sought to improve and update our training standards and the required course content kept changing. We grew also by liaison with local educational establishments. One example of this was better links with Gloucester College of Art and Technology. They generously loaned us their video equipment. We went on to use a lot of videoed role play. Through this method, trainers and students alike could see the extent to which counselling skills and theory was being integrated and worked out in role-played counselling sessions. As we grew in assessment skills, self-awareness and trust, new potential counsellors could gain confidence. They saw and heard themselves and others in action – and could learn ways to improve and gain confidence in the process. Through the national "Open College Network" we met similar training teams who were affiliated at various academic levels. Thist sharpened our minds about training methods and content. We were always conscious that standards and course material could easily fall

behind ever-advancing progress in counselling theory and pre-
sentation. I am proud that we managed to achieve Accreditation
in both the ACC and the Open College systems. After some
nine years our constantly changing course was taken by two of
our trainers, Neil and Sarah Jones to Worcester (some 30 miles
away) to enable their "Bridge" service to be founded similar to
Listening Post. Their first Director was another of our counsellors, Sue Cockeram. I knew her to be a first rate Christian
Counsellor, and was delighted with this lovely development.
(This service also still flourishes some 20 years later.)

We were also glad to have a relationship with Redcliffe Bible
College in Gloucester and this helped greatly after my retirement to raise academic standards. With a new Director in Sheila
Appleton, new agendas emerged – and I am very pleased that
the service has continued stronger. Like St. Paul we planted,
but Apollos watered [64.] and it was God who made it grow. All
praise to Him.

Summing up the story so far.

These diverse groups of like-minded Christians had found
common shared aims and visions. We had become increasingly
more aware of other services that were sprouting up all over the
country, and it was exciting! The news was getting around. Each
service had to keep the momentum of training counsellors going
to match the demand for new services. In Gloucestershire, we
soon had three centres. (See Appendix 1 for the timescale.)

Within a year of the formation of the Association of Christian
Counsellors in 1992 there were 51 member organisations on the
"Council of ACC". There seemed to be such a wealth of shared
knowledge and experience. By 1993 the "Board" seemed to
have grown too large. It seemed important to hone it down to
keep only those on the Board people who had specific roles.
This presented me with a quandary. I wanted to stay in the
team, but would have to leave if I did not find a role. Here came
another time when I found myself going in at "the deep end",
and offering to take on the only remaining job. I prayed that God
would enable me to fill the role of Publicity Co-ordinator. This

stretched my skill knowledge, but I did then become Newsletter Editor for six years from Autumn 1994. It was a challenging and most rewarding job. God seemed to have used a lot of us planting, and it was exciting to see the fresh shoots everywhere. We sought to encourage, inspire, educate, and inform those new services across the British Isles, then across Europe and linking across the world . ACC was most concerned from the outset about standards.

Individuals and groups were enabled to build up resource files, and develop systems which would lead towards "Accreditation" to standards devised and tested by ACC. Courses were advertised and books reviewed. During those 6 years the magazine grew from 16 pages in monochrome, up to 32 pages in full colour with over 4000 copies being produced 3 or 4 times per year. I thank God for many people who wrote articles, and especially for a lovely Christian printer in Gloucester **(Keith Creighton)** who, got it out so efficiently.

Keith is an amazingly gifted man who has never been daunted by his disablement. He started a national ministry to truckers called "Glory Road Ministries" and opened a Christian bookshop in 2010, when many others were closing. He designed some lovely covers for "ACCord". To be at the hub of ACC during these fertile years was a constant thrill. As I turn back the pages of that magazine I celebrate the lovely Christians we met, many of whom I could introduce in print. We held some memorable conferences – usually at Swanwick, Derbyshire. It was there that I "sat at the feet of" **Selwyn Hughes, Joyce Huggett, Gary Collins** and many others who symbolised the extremes of theological stances, who all had Christian Caring as their main enthusiasm.

Another inspiring series of Inter denominational Conferences (with Network as one of the leading services) called "Continuing the Journey" provided opportunities to learn from Counsellors and Pastoral workers with a different spread of Christian Spirituality. Here I was enthralled and enriched by a Jesuit priest, **(Father Gerard Hughes)**, an Anglican Nun (**Sister Margaret Magdalen**), and a Christian sex therapist (Moy Gill) and many others. My personal Christian horizons were widened enormously, as we shared meals, prayers, conversation, worship and inspiring seminars. Such people challenged my thinking (probably my prejudices too) and I sought to share this through ACCord and, of course, in Listening Post. [65]

Serving Bruised Pilgrims

Sister Margaret Magdalen was the head of Anglican convents in Wantage, England, and in South Africa. She contributed a surprisingly enriching dimensions to Christian Counsellor Conferences. Her book **"The hidden face of Jesus"** exhibits great insight and understanding of our Lord, especially in his adolescence, healing, confronting, suffering and his servant heart. That two Directors of Listening Post after David Walker spent time training in St. Marys in Wantage enriched the spirituality of that service.

The author of **"God of surprises"** surprised me by the depth of his Spirituality. I was glad to hear him at Christian Counselling Conferences. **Father Gerard Hughes** was nothing like I expected a Jesuit priest to be. He taught about prayer and meditation as a man who has looked at a hurting world asking "O God WHY?". He wrote that book **"for bruised pilgrims."** He showed a resilient faith. Jesus loves evangelicals – and priests who walk and talk with Him – and LISTEN to Him. Christian Counselling needs all these dimensions of faith.

ACC Conferences were enriched by two-day sessions such as **"Space for God"** led by **Joyce and David Huggett**. Joyce is best known for her lovely devotional books such as **"Open to God"**, **"The smile of Love"** and **"Finding God in the Fast Lane"**. She tackled with sensitivity issues of helping people reflect on finding peace beyond **"Anger and Conflict."**

In fact, the Listening Post Supervisors held a training weekend at St. Mary's Convent, Wantage (which was the Anglican convent whence Margaret Magdalen came) Two of our supervisors had spiritual roots there – whilst others seemed more at home with the Evangelical Alliance. My inspiration was coming from the spirituality of all these branches of God's Kingdom. When one day I get to the gates of Paradise, I do not expect St. Peter to demand my Methodist Membership Card, nor my Baptismal Certificate, but I do look forward to being surrounded by the "Peace which passes all understanding". This was shown in great measure through the hundreds who I was privileged to meet on these travels. More than once, I heard Brian Thorne[66], who carefully described himself as "A Christian in Counselling" (rather than a Christian Counsellor). Not only did he write most knowledgeably about Carl Rogers' "Client-centred Counselling", but he gave glimpses of Julian of Norwich's teachings, and the healing within the Finchden Manor Community. He recalled that George Lyward of Finchden emphasized that "The Holy Spirit is at work through wounded souls." Brian Thorne commended listening like Carl Rogers, and waiting on the Holy Spirit like Lyward, and staying close to the "Motherheart of God" like Mother Julian . We all learned so much from such a rich variety of the Saints in God's rainbow Kingdom.

In Part Four I will offer nine stories of people who were counselled through Listening Post. In more than one of these, the counsellors just had to provide a safe environment, and prayerfully listen patiently for the available healing of the Holy Spirit to be evident in the peace which was received in their lives in God's Time. Of course it was more complicated than that. For me the original logo of Listening Post said so much. The inspiration for the logo came from the cover of "A silence and a shouting" [6]which had a lonely bird on a telegraph wire, We placed two birds listening to each other with the wires going to the Cross. This was summed up by three lovely books by Joyce Huggett: Listening to God, Listening to Others, and finding Freedom.

So it was through the **Board of ACC** that I saw great devotion to raising standards of Training and Supervision. ACC Conferences provided a series of opportunities for Christian

Counsellors and Pastoral Workers to grow through learning from each other and from the cream of God's caring servants. Here were experts who commanded respect in the secular world but were also known well to Christians for their devotional works. I was astounded, privileged and inspired beyond measure to meet and sit at the feet of a panoply of modern-day saints. Many of these are listed in the Bibliography[68] Do glance at them – and Praise God with me for the Pioneers of Christian Counselling!

Part Four

~

31. Counselling on the edge, Together.

*M*ost counselling in Listening Post has been carried out in one-to-one counselling in interview rooms. However, the 9 true stories which are being offered in this book were nearly all examples of one "client" being counselled by a pair of counsellors. I hope that these true stories give you a taste of what we were trying to do in the early days of this new service. In these instances, I chose to be one of the counsellors and worked with a different female colleague on each "case". This helped us to grow as a counselling team and to appreciate each other's strengths and specialist knowledge or skills. Most of the principles of Counselling (eg. listening skills) are obviously identical. However, where initial assessment indicated a complicated or difficult set of presenting problems, then the old adage "two heads are better than one" frequently applied. In the early days, we found that we were often "counselling on the edge". There were some whose presenting problems seemed "a bit scary" to new counsellors. We did not want to turn too many potential "clients" away, but for those fresh out of training some presented seemingly insuperable issues. Read on and you will quickly get the flavour of what I mean. For many people needing help it takes great courage to seek it, especially when they feel that their world is collapsing around them and doubts and fears are overwhelming. So, as I happened to be one of the more experienced of counsellors, we decided that I would initially work in such cases in partnership with another experienced counsellor or supervisor, with the client's agreement. As we did "counsel on the edge" together, we grew in knowledge and skill – often in new territory for both of us. Bearing in mind the boundaries of confidentiality, able to share some of the knowledge or the problems, and we were supervised by another member of the Supervision Team. The stories which are included in this book are all in that category. I have been grateful to my counselling colleagues from their time spent sharing their memories. In most instances it has been wonderful to actually meet with the "client" several years after the event. That many of these people have given their stories in writing or on tape is very special. I am extremely grateful to them. In all except one they have given their written agreement to use the material, and directions as to how we should change their identity to protect confidentiality. (The exception was a person who died some years after counselling ended. "Katie's" healing from a multitude of complicated problems was one of the clearest example of the transforming power of the Love of God. Katie had separately told both counsellors that we could share this amazing true story. Katie was so grateful for the healing, and gave God all the glory – so do we!) Life goes on after counselling, and included in these stories are a few which exemplify the theme of Charles Swindoll's best-seller "Three steps forward and One back". [69]

This book is called "Together" because, in every instance. these stories continue with others taking the counselling story through and beyond "the edge". It often took courage and steps of faith, but the reward often gave a new understanding of God's Mathematics on our journey of life. Any of you who have walked a cliff-top or a mountain pass will know just how the fear and wonder of "walking on the edge" can be awesome especially when, you climb out of the depths and find anew the hope and promise of God-given mountain-top experiences.

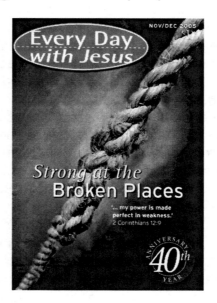

As I recalled these stories I recalled many times the edition of "Everyday with Jesus" Bible reading notes written by Selwyn Hughes in 2005, towards the end of his earthly life, entitled **"Strong at the broken places" Every one of these people felt broken in some way, and through the counselling they found new strength. Where I have quoted scripture in this section it has been that included in those notes Thank you CWR for permission to include that most explicit of pic-**

tures and to Selwyn Hughes for the daily inspiration from Scripture which has been my Daily Bread for over thirty years.

32. On the edge of being beaten by fear. Carol Lyn's Story

What motivates people to pluck up the courage to seek counselling help?

It is nearly always deeply unsettling feelings which dominate a person's thinking and behaviour and make them seek help to change. This is spelt out very well in Dr. Henry Cloud's book "Changes that heal (How to understand your past to ensure a healthier future)". [70] I commend this book most warmly, and wish I had read it earlier. Feelings cause worry and influence our behaviour, but they can be changed. FEAR is induced by threatening experiences, many of which often happened in childhood when we are least equipped to deal with them. There are, however, several helpful books which point us to ways of seeking and finding help and renewed hope.

One such is "Love is a choice" [71] from which I often quoted on our training courses. I had learnt through Probation that I did not have to like the actions of offenders – but I could still choose to love and help them.

Many times we helped people most by "Caring enough to confront" [72] even by helping them to confront either an abuser, or the debilitating fears left behind and held deeply in memory banks of feelings by the actions of the abuser, or the threats implicit in a fear-producing incident. It takes great courage to confront these feelings, and much sensitivity on the part of the counsellors.

Many books on dealing with fears and phobias talk of "progressive desensitisation" or "flooding" – and we commended careful use of such techniques in counselling. "Carol Lyn" was a young Christian who sought our help with one crippling fear, and Sue consulted me when she was requested to help her friend. (Sue was already a very competent Counsellor and in later years went on to found "The Bridge Christian Counselling

Service" in Worcester which stemmed out of Listening Post Training.)

We chose to use some methods which many counsellors would find unusual, but decide for yourself when you read Carol Lyn's story. She wrote the following in 2010.

My dog phobia.
I have always been afraid of dogs. Being born in India, my earliest experience was of my uncle who had several dogs. Every day after school the dogs would greet me, and I would climb the nearest gate or wall to get away from them. Most of my childhood experience with dogs was negative. Trying to run away from them, feeling anxious and full of fear as I was doing this. Dogs filled me with great fear and anxiety.
(Carol later told us of two occasions when the dogs attacked her. Once a big one sat on her head and she feared it would smother her.)

When God called me to India (as a missionary) it concerned me that I had such a fear. So I decided to get some counselling. I had found out that Christian Counselling had just started in Gloucester. Therefore I decided to see if I could nail this phobia. At my first visit at the centre I found out that my friend Sue was working there as a Counsellor. We had been friends for years, and she informed me that she had just got a puppy. It was decided that with David Walker and Sue would try and break this fear.

(Carol felt safe with Sue, and we chose to meet initially in my home because I had a cuddly collie dog who was loved by all the locals. We affirmed our mutual faith – and I noted she wore a cross.)

We initially prayed, and I remember David saying "You have a cross around your neck." "Hold it as your reminder that God is with you – always"

This helped me a lot, as I realised that God would give me the strength to face the fear. David also assured me that I would be in control and he would not let the situation be so overwhelming that I could not cope. This reassured me and trust Dave and Sue.

When I fetched my border collie, Stanley, on a lead into the room gently, I realised dramatically how deep was the terror. Carol leapt onto the settee shuddering! I got Stanley to sit or lie alongside me some feet from Carol. Stanley almost went to sleep. I sat on the floor and stroked him as we talked, and eventually Carol plucked up the courage to sit on the floor; and stroked him also for probably 15 minutes. We thanked God together and asked Him to stay with Carol as she met with us next in a week's time at Sue's home. The "progressive desensitisation" continued at Sue's home where she had placed her bouncy puppy in a baby's playpen. Here Carol could be in the same room and watch. Eventually she allowed herself to be harmlessly kissed on the hand by the puppy. Carol survived well. Sue very imaginatively lent her videos of dogs, to help her to see the positive enjoyment that people get in England from these pets. Then Sue took her puppy and Carol to "dog-training" (and dog-owners' training). Once again Carol survived it. Imagine it, she was surrounded by dogs being trained! This was what psychologists call "flooding"! Again she survived!

This process enabled me to trust the counsellors. It was a significant part of my healing. Over the weeks and months my confidence grew, and I felt more comfortable with the dogs. When eventually I returned to India I spent the first weeks (even months) overcoming my fear of another dog in the missions office. This dog was an alsation and several times tried to attack me. However, knowing God was with me, and my previous positive experiences with a dog enabled me to overcome this fear. My work was in the slums in India, and often if we were starting a new work I would be attacked by a dog. However I was never bitten or hurt. Fear of dogs no longer rules my life. I thank God that the counsellors' understanding and patience enabled me to do mission work and fulfil my calling.

"The Lord is my strength and shield" Psalm 28:8

Thank you, Carol Lyn, for having the courage and faith to choose to confront your fears and persevere with God's call on your life. Writing this book is worth it for this story alone – and there is more!

33. Climbing upwards, Three steps forward and two back John's Story

For more than 20 years I have had occasional contact with John. When he heard I was writing a book of memories, he offered to tell his story. He chose to do so on tape. At my home he spoke almost unprompted for three hours, and then we had a second session similarly at his home. For this I am very grateful. Right from the start of Listening Post, people in need were guided to us, often by Christians. We learnt lots of important lessons along the way, one being that God's process of challenge and change is not steady. Sometimes deep pain takes a long time to be healed, because it stems from deep hurts in childhood.

John could have been one such case, as he went through a long rocky "journey on the edge."We recalled how known John for over twenty years since Maureen and I counselled him together almost before the office was even open. He had heard we were in business, and he needed help. He was a Christian, but was really struggling. As his story poured out (more than twenty ago) it became clear that, in growing up, he had been desperate to be accepted by other teenagers. He was bullied so badly that he became a bully.At thirteen he was already an alcoholic, and had dabbled in drugs and the occult. Nevertheless he had managed to train as a teacher. John told us that he was married at twenty, and they had a daughter, His wife could not cope with his drinking. She left him, taking their daughter, which hit John hard. He felt he just could not stop himself hurting people, and he planned to kill himself. He thought heroin meant death so tried it. Somehow he wanted to be in groups yet found himself destroying relationships. Then he started drinking again in remorse – it was a vicious circle.

He was then befriended by a Christian teacher in the school. *("I loathed Christians")* She got him to go to counselling at one of the new Christian Counselling Services (which I knew well) He had buried his pride and sought help, probably thought he would lose his job. He knew that in his sober moments he was a competent teacher. He even taught RE – among other subjects. (My experience with addicts came in handy in these conversations, especially when he talked in AA concepts.) John's taped memories recall:

"I realised I could not do things myself" "Whilst in the grip of substances I ceased to have control over anything, least of all regulating intake. Alcohol was the thing I based my life on. It was my pain diminisher, gave me power and meaning, took away my sense of isolation and loneliness, guilt and shame"

From his early teens. John showed a lot of self-awareness, and an understanding that the behaviour that he described was destructive of relationships and often potentially violent, of which he was ashamed. In his good times he was a likeable and talented person, but he described how he had broken several expensive guitars in temper.

"I realised I had to change. I seemed to have a sort of death wish, wrecked my car and then my teaching career. My life became chaotic to the extent that I possessed only one bag and was homeless at about 25".

His mother picked him up several times, at least financially. Somehow he got on a 39 week Residential Rehabilitation Course, following the Alcoholics Anonymous programme. Many of the lessons from that programme went in deep. It was his addictive personality and life-style which needed to change. Then this teacher friend became a sort of Christian mentor from a distance at different times in his life, and although I never met her I knew she was always there for him as an anchor at crisis times. So it was two years after the AA experience that John arrived in Gloucester and sought counselling help. He never drank alcohol again (as far as we knew). If he did it was masked by other "over-the- counter drugs."

"These were destroying me." "I was in a place that was impossible, The feelings were bigger than I was."

He wanted to think his life-style through and find roots in this new area. Our feeling was that he needed a Christian church base. That seemed to be working out as, despite several stormy relationships, John eventually settled into a church, played guitar in their Praise Band, and he got married into a Christian family. My wife and I went to his wedding. It seemed idyllic. However, this too ended in divorce – and he sought our help again within a couple of years. I seemed to be brought into John's life several times over the next 18 years, normally at times of family celebration or crisis. The word "Together" symbolised for me that I was just part of God's team of carers for John, which included in turn several evangelical churches. In each of these John used his musical talents. Each fellowship welcomed him in, and nurtured him a bit further along towards the road to spiritual maturity which God intended. As John talked without prompting for three hours of tape-recording, I saw how he realised that many Christians had been there for him at many stages in his life. He saw how Jesus had been there too and was influencing those who sought to lovingly guide him. I knew that, in the past, I had sometimes held back deliberately from confronting his behaviour when it seemed irrational or even sinful. He knew just how manipulative he could be.

"I would just have run if you had confronted me more...." "But you did confront me – and also you enabled me to look at things I did not want to look at....I did have the choice to run or to stay. That is why I chose to go to a church where my problems would be prayed about, and that would leave God in charge. I

had always needed to be in control, or put addictive substances in control. In AA terms I was really claiming God as my Higher Power...."" I had done things since Listening Post that had put me in bondage again...You came to my wedding, saw me married to a Christian lady, saw me settled into a good teaching job, helped by a Christian Housing Association to buy our own house then...something happened – it all went wrong....my wife left me. I had not acted violently, nor started using again, nor been unfaithful! That struck me as darn unfair! I could not go anywhere with the pain. I was revoltingly angry. I went into school one morning and then could not read the words...and I could not plan a lesson. I could not think or read in sentences, and I was laid off with depressive illness. I never went back. I proceeded to get virus after virus – an 'ME' sort of weakness, staggered around with a hurt back. This lasted the best part of a couple of years. So it was four years ago I started taking codeine-based pain-killers again and within six months I got 'conflicty'; playing computer games; using a lot of coffee ; chain-smoking; sleeplessness, paranoia, fears about loneliness, and rejection. It was out of control, and it got worse." "However, I do feel that God has got me on a short rein, My dependence on drugs has remarkably changed to a dependence on Him. Knowing I was back in bondage to painkillers. I called out to God –'I just want to want not to want this' God had HEARD! He took it away!" "I found my marriage heart again – and a new partner on the journey – with 'Victoria'... We have been encouraged by our church to seek help to walk along this path together....We went to a Healing Centre together - and God is helping us both rebuild our lives...." "I still mess up, but I have this Christian Family to help me restore " "It was patient listening and prayer about anger, hurt, and pain. We placed all that had happened in God's hands. I heard God saying 'Don't take anti-depressants' and I did not. We asked God to help find the way - and He did. Pain and anger continued – but I was able to use the gift of music and photography. God knew I needed encouragement...and it was GOOD!" Through my new Christian Fellowship I found friends I could trust. They laid hands on me and prayed for me. My dependence on drugs and self has changed to dependence on Him. Once again God has given me a marriage heart – but He is saying 'Not Yet'. I do not have that tornado in the brain now – and "Victoria" went to the Christian Healing Centre for counselling and ministry with me. I felt I was being held by God. Like Lazarus I have been healed from death. For me it was from anger. I had to let go of control. I was shown my false beliefs.

Now in 2010 John some things had really changed. He has taken another "Three steps forward", The question remains as to whether he will take "two steps back". I recently prayed with him with his new Christian Church Family; I heard his new Biblical ways of thinking. It shows how he has really sought to put God in control in his life. Moses learnt many times on his long journey across the Wilderness that when we reach out to God, He never lets go of us.

"And God said 'I will be with you@ and this will be a sign..." Exodus3:11

34. On the edge of brokenness – Martha's Jigsaw

As I thought about these examples of Christian counselling, "Martha" sprang to mind. She had written her story – and lots of poems which showed great sensitivity, insight and compassion. Martha was one who demonstrated the kind of personal situation which frequently comes to counselling services. She had been sailing through life seemingly "normally" when three things threw her off balance. "All change is crisis" says one book I quoted earlier, but when a close relative dies, your oldest daughter leaves home, and you move house all at same time we all could feel like Martha. She went "over the edge" and felt she was "*cracking up*".

"It reminded me of when I got married and my grandmother was ill. They kept from me that she had died (wanting to spare me). I resented it greatly that I could not go to her funeral. What else could happen? Then years later things seemed to go wrong

again. I felt really low. My friendly neighbour was training to be a Christian Counsellor and she suggested I go to Listening Post.

The counsellor had introduced Martha to me to get help to decide how best to help her. Martha told me she was a Christian and was feeling really low and worthless. She remembered that we had listened to her story, and I had assured her that "God never made any junk". She had been well made and would recover. She told us she had postnatal depression, and got into the habit of constantly checking things. She went to the Samaritans years ago, wanting to feel whole again, not broken and fragile – like that jigsaw she was struggling to do. I asked if, unusually, I could visit the counsellor and Martha, in her home. (It reminded me of my days in Probation when I discovered so much about people on home visits.) Sure enough, in that comfortable home my eyes lighted on the massive jigsaw she had put aside under the sideboard in frustration. Martha explained,

"What a beautiful castle! It was the dark edges that stopped me making progress." We discussed how the box showed the promise of the picture – even though it was broken. Martha went on *"Just like my life. You coaxed me to finish it and we prayed that God would heal my brokenness too! You suggested I give up focussing on the dark bits, but concentrate on the familiar bits of the castle and see if it would come together better.* **'and pray about it as you go'** *you added."*

"I did just that. It still took a week. These scriptures really spoke to me during this time 'You will know the truth and the truth will set you free' (John 8)

'My power is greatest when you are weak' (2 Corinthians 12)

'God is able to do so much more than we can ever ask for or even think of'(Ephesians3)

Slowly I started to struggle less, and as I worked on the nice things I recognised the dark bits began to fit."

One evening I got that phone call - ***"I've finished it!"*** "Great!" I said. "Now find some hardboard and **glue it down!**"It all took time, but in later years, Martha thanked God for His "Amazing Grace" and faithfulness as she recalled how she had managed to sit with her father as he edged towards death, helped her mother through Alzheimers' disease, survived her son leaving home, enjoyed grandchildren, trained as a Christian Counsellor, and helped others cope with the ups and downs of life. I thank God for her persistent neighbour who was always there when needed, and for giving her the insights and real lasting Peace

"Therefore, do not worry about tomorrow…each day has enough trouble of its own"
Matt 6:34

35. On the edge of a chaotic abyss. Samuel's story.

Samuel was one whom I took on alone, because what he presented when he came to Listening Post he presented symptoms that made me instantly doubt whether we could help him. He seemed severely mentally ill. Yet here was a young man who said he was a Christian. He came to us because we were Christians and at least he was glad that I sat him down and listened. As he entered my room he was careful not to shake hands. I started the conversation by saying that it must have been hard for him to get to us. Slowly his story began to emerge. He seemed terrified of everything. He would not walk on pavements in case he was contaminated by bushes or walls or other people. He did go to church and sat at the back. His wide vocabulary told me he was very intelligent, but irrationally scared.

By the end of an hour I assessed that the best way forward initially would be to go back to my old Probation days, and see him in his home. He desperately needed to feel safe. He said he would be grateful for that. He was clearly rejecting of doctors, despite displaying symptoms of mental illness. Nonetheless, he had plucked up the courage to come to a Christian Counselling Service and I must not be another person to reject him. A few days later we resumed counselling in his dark and chaotic flat. He showed me to an armchair which was surrounded on the floor by dirty mugs containing .used teabags. Other people must have visited him. His bookshelves spoke volumes. The books were higgledy piggledly resting on shelves. The few titles that were showing said that he was a language student. Sam told me his story slowly. He was *"a real failure"*. I said I did not think that was true, as I picked up a book that was in Russian. Slowly it leaked out that he had a first class Honours BA in Russian, but he had had his MA thesis rejected. This had shattered him. He allowed me to pray that the Lord show us His Way forward. When he offered me a cup of tea my Probation training made me remember the warnings we were given about accepting tea in dirty homes. I cringed within and said "Only when we have washed up all these mugs, together".

(Another major reason for the title of this book, is that I have long firmly believed that you can never impose help on someone, but when they ask for it then it can only become effective for them, if done "**Together**")

We agreed that he wanted his life to get back into some sort of order – and I commented that "I really would love to see that bookshelf in order - because it tells me that God had given you a good brain, and wants me to help you start using it again as He intended". (It turned out Samuel could speak at least 4 languages). Next week the shelves were semi tidy – at least my assessment was beginning to prove right. I gave him a copy of a book which I knew to be really helpful. It was entitled "A Practical Workbook for the Depressed Christian" by John Lockley. [74]

It began –
"Being a Christian does not guarantee immunity from depression, and being depressed does not mean that your beliefs are rendered invalid. God loves you as you are, unconditionally." "Could I ask you to read this book, please, so it can represent a sort of agenda for our work together. I believe that God will help you choose which chapters are relevant to you – and it

will help us both." (I have learnt over the years to "use fire to fight fire" and that often the problem situation which a person exhibits could also give a hint to the method of helping.) To cut a long story short, Samuel did read a chapter each week and he told me what it taught him. (It was rather like a college tutorial – which he and I had both experienced) It helped him to choose chapters which he knew related to him, and skip others. In the process I affirmed that he was gaining insight, and regaining his coping mechanisms, tackle the great fear, to face down the "failure" and the unfairness that he felt about that. After some weeks I began to feel quite hopeful that he too was gaining in hope. Really he just needed someone alongside him in his loneliness. And I had offered to walk the path towards "normality" with him. We brought our Healing Creator alongside us on that journey by bracketing our sessions with prayer. He seemed to value this, and I did check out at every stage that I was not imposing anything upon him. He recognised that he needed structure in his life and here we were working within a helpful therapeutic system, designed by John Lockley, but encouraging him to do all the application of his life himself. Eventually, we made a bargain. Having assured myself that his MA submission would be in English, I offered to proof-read it, if and when he plucked up the courage to rewrite it. Soon the first few pages emerged – and I could read and understand them and I was genuinely impressed with them. The pages came at me week by week faster than I could read them – and we had interesting discussions. (Especially when he wrote about a Russian poet who had been so depressed that he threatened to kill himself in a duel. I had to assure myself that he was not going to emulate this poet! At this time I felt like the TV demonstrators who say "don't try this at home", and shared that with him. He saw the logic, and we agreed that the poet did not have our saving God to fall back on!) Eventually, he did re-submit his MA Thesis, and we awaited the outcome! In the meantime he completed a "TEFL" (Teaching English as a Foreign Language) Course. This really got him back into the real world where he was accepted by fellow students and teachers, as well as by Christians. We then talked about – "What next?" In panic he had a flight back into instability. There was something in his background which so far he had not revealed to me. It related to the MA failure, which made him certain that he must live away for Britain so he could make a fresh start.

"I think I'll go to teach abroad...Iceland, France, or Germany, or Rumania or Russia or Japan or SPAIN" (He was carried away by wanting to reject Britain – as if that would sort him out. "But you can't speak Icelandic or Japanese or Spanish ?" I challenged. *"Well I'll learn Spanish. then!"* And he did! In three months – and worked there teaching English as a Foreign Language – and learning other languages en route. And he did gain his Masters Degree – and can walk on pavements without fear. He remained in correspondence with me. I sent him "Everyday with Jesus" Bible Reading Notes which I had shared was my daily Christian stable diet.
(Until he was nurtured by a Spanish Christian mentor in an Evangelical Church)

Samuel will always be different. Recently he sent me a video by email praising God that he was able to go to a gym. There he was dancing on the video dressed as a green gorilla! "God loves even green gorillas who love Him" – and Jesus healed untouchables on the Sabbath!

"Jesus sent him away saying 'Return home, and tell how much God has done for you'". Luke 8:39

36. On the edge of running amok. Joanne's Story

In the early days of a new Listening Post centre, Christine was asked to see a new client. Christine remembers clearly the anger which seemed to overwhelm this lady who admitted quite freely that she came to us, recommended by her church. However, it was her rage which worried her. Quite sensibly Christine asked me to join her in counselling, because in training I had talked about anger and domestic violence. This lady, whom we will call "Joanne" had a tale which would concern any counsellor. Joanne had been a heavy drinker since she was a teenager. She had 3 brothers and a sister, and all of them had been beaten and bullied by their belligerent father. Additionally he had chosen Joanne (then aged ten) to rape. She feared and hated him for this. The other children did not seem to realise about her being raped (or perhaps it was happening to them sometimes also?) Joanne despised her mother for not protecting her. Joanne had been in mental hospital for "detoxification treatment" Whilst there she became really distressed by a male patient who seemed intent on pestering her. When Joanne reported this to a female nurse, instead of protection. The nurse's retort was "TOUGH! Get on with it!"

This was a red rag to Joanne, who packed her bags and discharged herself. She made a formal written complaint to the Hospital authorities. Joanne thought this had been ignored. Like many alcoholics' reactions to problems, Joanne got drunk. She then made abusive phone calls to the nurse at the Alcohol Treatment Unit, eventually threatening to KILL her.

"I wanted her to feel the fear I had felt. I reached out for the vodka and rang again. Two nice policemen came and arrested me. They charged me with "threats to kill" and I was released with a Caution."

Recalling this with Joanne several years later, she remembered being recommended to Listening Post by Christian friends.

"I was glad to be seen by two counsellors. Each time you listened to me sympathetically, and did not judge me, even though I told you about my real RAGE and resentments and hurts. You asked if we could end each session with some prayer. This seemed to let me go away calmer, putting the anger in God's hands. You were nothing like my parents. You listened without being shocked when I told you about my home life, my anger and resentments. My faith did help me, and having understanding friends. Through counselling I had at last found that sharing my thoughts and feelings was not wrong. I was encouraged to seek

*specialised help again, and got financial aid from my church to go to Nelson House. This is one of 200 self-help organisations which focus on the AA Twelve Step Programme. This left a lasting impression on my ways of thinking. After I admitted my need of a Higher Power, I had to make a list of people I had harmed. Then I needed to become willing to make amends, and humbly ask God to help me to remove my short- comings. That was a long list, absorbed over several weeks in Residential setting, and in groups. It really got into our systems. Above all, I needed to have the courage to **practice forgiveness** towards my father and even that nurse. **This was HARD**, but when we talked about how to do it, I was helped to regain peace of mind.I couldn't think of anything left to resent. I became content. I still get angry, Who doesn't? But I don't need the alcohol to deal with it.They said - 'Admit it, own it, let it go! ' and I did!*

Since then I have had some ups and downs. These are mostly financial. David, you went the 'Second Mile' when the Council took me to a Tribunal. You said to me 'Do not say much' " (I did not need to) "I surprised myself that I was able to give a good account, and did not get angry. It was important to me that I got a good hearing. Although they made me repay some money they treated me sympathetically.

I remember counselling because the counsellors seemed to care, accepted me, and recognised that I wanted to get better and. I even ring them up occasionally, mainly to tell them a joke. What a relief to have a laugh instead of rage and worry!!!

Pause for thought.

It has been a pleasure to know Joanne, I will always remember when I told her that a heron had stripped most of my goldfish from the pond. Her response was to give me a lovely painting of the heron on trial. He was standing in the dock with a fish tucked under his and the bewigged Judge wagging fingers of scorn at him. That picture hangs in my conservatory within sight of the pond, reminding me that the best way to deal with annoyance is to laugh and go on regardless. Mary's joke book has several attributable to Joanne. When I passed her a copy of Greta Randle's lovely book "Forgiving the impossible" [74] her response was to share the lovely letter she had written to God about forgiveness. That cost her, but it also gave great relief. It contained some really important conclusions that I suspect no one told her directly. Especially she recognised how spending her life hating and mistrusting other people was a form of self-protection — but *"it left me a very solitary existence, trying to drink away the negatives did drown out everything good. What a mess!""I drank to feel heavenly and experienced hell!" "Where my Dad was concerned, I wanted to be loved, I was hurt instead. I held onto the anger and resentments and pain. They festered inside me for years because I did not talk about it. I kept people at a distance as a way of protecting myself from future harm… So Dad, you don't belong in my head anymore. I am handing you over to God who is compassionate and wise. I am also handing over the anger and hatred I felt for you. Whatever happened in the past is forgiven. I neither need nor want to dwell on it. Nurse C, I forgive you. It's over. Live in peace. May God also forgive me. Where there once was hatred and anger please fill me with goodness."*

I thank Joanne for sharing those important thoughts with us. The Lord has heard her prayer and is already richly blessing her. He has unlocked her artistic talent, and she is painting well again — even planning to exhibit some pictures. Her only son and his wife give her a lot of pleasure. Her family are demonstrating new dimensions of Love. I pray that she will keep on filling her home with beauty and laughter — and prayer. We pray that her words of witness may help others. When Joanne rings me at 9pm I used to fear she was under the influence of vodka. Now it is to tell Mary or me a joke. It is so much better to laugh together. The Edinburgh Festival Fringe exhibition "Jesus Laughing and loving", toured the UK. These portraits of the Humour of Jesus showed that Jesus was really the life and soul of the party. I love the title of Charles Swindoll's lovely book, inspired by St. Paul's letter from Prison to the Phillipians.

"Maybe it's time to laugh again and experience OUTRAGEOUS JOY" [75]

"Jesus said: 'I have come that they might have life, and have it to the full'" John10:10

37. Obsessed by Prayer, Robbie's story

"Robbie" wrote an extremely detailed account, only as one who has suffered from OCD would do. I have used his words, rather like a "Readers Digest" condensed version. *After spending the first 37 years of my life in Glasgow, and following a promotion at work, I moved to Gloucester in 1987. My wife and son were part of the move. We took the usual personal effects, plus some invisible personal baggage, namely my Obsessional compulsive disorder (OCD) OCD is more than checking and rechecking and washing and rewashing. OCD is a disabling, life-limiting and exhausting illness that is capable of reducing an individual to a state in which they are almost unable to function. This is no laughing matter for the person concerned, nor their loved ones. From a Christian perspective, it most certainly denies the fullness of life offered by Jesus – as announced by John.* [76] *OCD came on me suddenly in 1969. Whilst on holiday in a guesthouse, late at night, alone in my bedroom, I had read a short passage from my Bible and, for a reason unknown to me, I found myself compelled to read it over and over again. The reading and re-reading continued for over an hour. This was a harbinger of what took a hold of my mind, insidiously or subtly, until 1976 (the year our only child was born). In my case, the compulsion was PRAYER – the same very long prayer, which (with Variations) had to be "said" (usually in my head) repeatedly until I got it word perfect. This ritual had to be gone through before I could attempt any new activity which even remotely gave me pleasure. My logical mind knew these to be simply empty rituals. When I consulted my doctor, he referred me to a psychiatrist.*

When medicines proved ineffective, the psychiatrist suggested electro convulsive therapy (ECT). My wife, as my advo-

cate, rejected this out of hand. The downward spiral continued during the eight weeks in the psychological department of a University medical school. With the help of the psychologist I was enabled to manage life better. Perhaps unsurprisingly the move to new things in Gloucestershire in 1988 brought about the old ways of Obsessional praying. My OCD was back with a vengeance! But this time I was a stranger in a new town – and my whole support network had gone. The new job was stressful. So it was in 1988 that I met David Walker. He too was in a new role as a Lay Worker in the Methodist Church. At least he had an inkling of what OCD was about, but acknowledged that he could only walk the journey with me as a friend whilst I sought medical help again. So a psychiatrist gave me medication and referred me for psychotherapy, who used Cognitive behaviour therapy (CBT). After no discernible progress, David accompanied me at what was to be my final session with the therapist. When she declared that she was discharging me as there seemed to be no progress, David declared his confidence that TOGETHER we would seek the help of our Creator God – who had made all things good. This gave me some hope – even though we were "truly flying by the seat of our pants."

David told me that he discussed this situation with both David Bick his mentor, and Vernon Godden his Supervisor together they had advised a short "Desert experience". So I agreed to abstain from all Christian activities – even reading the Bible. This period was marked by a very informal celebration of Communion conducted by Vernon Godden. The following 6 weeks were almost compulsion-free. Oh, what bliss! As a way of coming out of the desert, I spent a few days at the monastic guesthouse at Prinknash Abbey, near Gloucester. These beautiful grounds in the Cotswolds exuded Peace. David Bick, my "Spiritual Director" saw me for 20 minutes each day. I had expected some heavyweight spiritual exercises. However, he just asked me to enjoy the surroundings. There was to be no analysing what I saw, and no trying to spiritualise things. My Spiritual Director offered me just one verse from Psalm 46:10

"Be still and know that I am God"

I must have repeated these eight words differently hundreds of times – as only a OCD sufferer can – with every imaginable change of emphasis as I just stood and stared and enjoyed the Creator's wonder. I felt a real PEACE. So I was "allowed" to attend worship......... even mid-week services at Harnhill Healing Centre. But the OCD crept back in. I invented new "must do" compulsion. Things seemed bleak again.But David never let me lose hope.

We "hung on in there". We had tasted a hint of hope so we decided to try again. SO *In 1993 I entered "the desert" for a second time, but on this occasion it was for six months. As before, a Celebration of Communion marked my entry into the desert.*

Pause for thought.

For "Robbie" again Prayer was off limits, but a small trusted group of Christians were praying for him regularly – asking God to "Teach us your Way" (Psalm 86:11). It is my long held belief that if we ask God with "underlined: undivided hearts" He will always answer your sincere prayers. In the spirit of Romans 8:37 we are destined to be "more than Conquerors". I was convinced that "Robbie" would inherit that promise just as I had done when, as a stuttering student, I had called out to Him in tears of desperation, in that phone box outside LSE – and was healed of my debilitating stammer!.The secret is to reach out and ask – and then trust God to heal, but always in His Way. So "Robbie" returned to Prinknash Abbey – and I spent a retreat with him. On this occasion Robbie taught me about Celtic Christianity and the "immanence"[76] of God. I felt that this put Creator God back in control of "Robbie's" life in HIS WAY, free from unnecessary compulsive rituals (which are not part of God's creative plan). We drew on "Robbie's" depth of knowledge of the lovely books of David Adam, [77] and drew him into the real protective Circle of Love which is so memorably described in Celtic symbolism.

This "Robbie" taught me whilst I learnt more of the healing which Jesus was ministering again in that peaceful environment. [78]

"It certainly spoke of a God who is close up and personal rather than a God who called the Universe into being and left humanity to get on with it. It spoke of a God who is interested in and close to me in every aspect of my life."

This again illustrates how effective counselling can be if we combine the three aspects which Joyce Huggett combines so helpfully in a combined volume of three of her books. "Listening to God, Listening to others, Finding Freedom" (TOGETHER).[79] Suffice it to say that in later years "Robbie" trained both as a preacher and as a Christian Counsellor, gained a BA (Hons) in Theology, and has worked in a Christian social work agency in his native Scotland. He ended his contribution to this book with the following words.

"Circle me Lord; Keep protection near; and danger afar.
Circle me Lord; Keep hope within; Keep doubt without.
Circle me Lord; Keep truth within; Keep compulsions out.
Circle me Lord; Keep peace within; Keep evil out." [80]

As I work with service users who are often homeless, addicted to alcohol or drugs, it seems odd to me that God uses one with such a history of another form of addiction caring for others with addiction problems. ***"Talk about a wounded healer!"***

38. "Counselling on the edge of rejection"
Squaring the Circle of Abuse
Katie's Story

We were on the edge of saying we could not counsel this person as soon as we knew how complicated were the facts given to us by the Christian Social Worker who was bringing "K...." to us. Frankly the Social Services Department felt that "K...." needed much more than they could offer him/her. And so it proved. I remember having doubts about accepting this young man who was dressed as a woman. However I could not imagine who would accept him if we turned him away. I asked Ann to work with me because she had some specialist experience which might help. She readily agreed. Simply listening to this apparently confused person moved me considerably especially as he eventually described the abuse by his mother's "partner", for which the man was sent to prison. On release the mother had this man back home. Therefore, for the protection of the child "K" had to go into Care. (Which is probably where the social worker got involved) How K.... got back with his mother I do not know. "K" was very forgiving, because he had had several "father figures " in his life. Nevertheless "K" was clearly wanting to find peace with the real person God had created. He wanted to call himself by a female name. I usually used the female name he chose, as that represented his greatest desire, but Ann used the male name "K" by which his mother knew him. Right from the outset we two counsellors often referred to him as "Katie", when we talked or even prayed for him/her affectionately. "Katie" lived with all three names because they represented the mixed up one life which we got to know very well. Our aim was to help Katie to find peace and wholeness with the God whom we all three worshipped. We always prayed that our Creator please show us the way forward. We remembered that He had brought one world out of chaos and could bring oneness to this life eventually. Katie desperately wanted to get beyond this duality. Together we read Ecclesiastes 3:11 with the promise that "He will make everything beautiful in its time", and prayed that God would enable us to find His Peace in His time. Somehow Katie had gained a Hebrew Bible – greatly thumbed and underlined. This was often brought out in our discussions. When we were seeking God's Way forward this seemed a good starting point. There proved to be more complications than we had ever imagined, as we discovered that in the past Katie had been a server in a witch's coven, and was addicted to heroin. We were very conscious of a feeling of evil in the home, where we met weekly and during each visit we had a group of trusted friend covering our discussions with prayer. Katie had been seeking to have a sex-change operation, but had been told by a London specialist that he had to live as a female consistently for 2 to 3 years before the operation could be contemplated. We focussed on Katie's faith as a "Messianic Jew" and promised to stick with him/her through this journey of discovery. It was often a bumpy ride, but it began with Katie forgiving his/her mother for what had seemed like rejection. Katie was supplied by the local addiction unit with needles and was injecting methadone liquid (which is normally taken my mouth) several times each day. Yet Katie wanted to stop, and decided to call upon God in sung prayer with the guitar each time he/she longed to "fix" the drug. Eventually this battle was won! Katie reported progressively the desire was lessening. Our role seemed to encourage and support with prayer. We also prayed regularly there and from home against the evil and for God to rule in Katie's life. Katie learnt in this way to put God first in her life, and to pray for His constant guidance. "The truth will set you free – and then you will be free indeed" said Ann. Note 81

Some of this praying against the remnants of occultic evil in Katie's life was new territory for me and once again I was "counselling on the edge of my knowledge" with Ann who was more experienced in this respect than me. However, I had often felt the presence of evil in Parkhurst Prison as I sat in the cells of convicted paedophiles, rapists, or murderers. Here it was different. We were alongside a Christian victim of terrible abuse. He/she was seeking freedom from addiction, the wounds of occultic abuse and conflict over sexual identity. It was beyond the edge of our competence or experience as Christian Counsellors, but we both had great faith that Jesus never called someone without giving them the spiritual equipment for the job. Gradually, over many months Katie learnt to fight the overwhelming desire to "fix" (inject) the methadone. Amazingly, a local church welcomed "her" into their Praise Group and I attended an evening Praise service at Katie's request. This ordinary Christian group (who knew something of the turmoil of this mixed up person) offered love and acceptance in a way he/she had never experienced before. The bondages had been broken and freedom was found at last. Our counselling lasted for over a year, but we gradually saw Katie less and less. Katie contacted Ann several times.

This seemed to confirm Ann's assurance that she should affirm the male side of this complicated person. "K" decided not to go ahead with the sex-change operation, grew a beard, and gained employment as a van driver. He also moved to a different church, with a male name. "K" died suddenly – but peacefully. I received an invitation from his church to attend a Celebration Service for the life of this child of God. It was well-attended, and clearly moved many of his friends. They did not know details of this complicated life story, "K" had witnessed continually to God's Healing Power. He played his guitar joyfully there often. We do thank God for healing this his broken child and taking him home. I praise God for these two Church Fellowships who welcomed this complicated and wounded person into their Fellowship, and surrounded him with LOVE. Jesus said we must love our neighbours as ourselves,

Let us remember He also said "Go, and do thou likewise."

"For Christ's sake I delight in weakness, in insults, in hardships, in persecution, in difficulties. For when I am weak, then I am strong" 2 Corinthians 12:10

39. On the edge of breakdown.

Pete wrote :

On reflection, I have always had this nagging feeling that there was something wrong with me. I felt that I'd spent my life disappointing everyone including my parents, teachers and myself. At school, I was bored and struggled to pay attention. I was told that I was bright and could do the work but my grades were low. Although I did enough to become a teacher in a special school, I now think my low self-esteem caused me to become overly sensitive to criticism. It brought back too many deep memories of 'failing', of being 'told-off for being naughty' and I was always very scared of being criticised. In fact if I was (or thought I might be), I found that I would be extremely defensive.

In 1995, the special school where I was teaching had failed its Ofsted inspection and I felt partly responsible. I was being criticised, my worst nightmare. The Head teacher was found to

be inadequate, and was removed from his post. Consequently, I found I was suffering a reactive depression for which my doctor signed me off work. I had already had several occurrences of depression, but my doctor did not feel I was adepressive as I always recovered very quickly once I had been removed from the situation. For support, insight and a hopeful healing of my reoccurring depression, I went to Listening Post, feeling I had failed. I soon found I was blessed with two gifted counsellors and it was an amazing experience to feel an unconditional acceptance. It was great to be able to pour out the pain and to know that my counsellors were actively listening to me. Looking back from fifteen years later, I can now see it was the beginning of the healing which has been an on-going experience as God has led me forward, has gradually rebuilt my self-belief and healed restrictive memories from the past. I feel I have been led out of teaching and have been running my own business for the past twelve years. God has also used my experience to share with several other men who have been going through troubled times. He isn't finished with me yet and I want to witness to His healing love to any who are going through a difficult time.

Reflective comment

Counselling Together in Listening Post when the two counsellors had differing Christian and educational backgrounds gave an important flavour to the work. June's experience of St. Mary's Anglican Convent in Wantage, and then as an Anglican Lay Reader on a large council housing estate, would seem to contrast with my Methodist heritage. However, we found much more upon which to agree than differ. It was a privilege to sit alongside Pete, as he found a new peace and to find in later years how even his painful journey could help others who lived through similar pain. God used his particular skills, honed at the educational "coal-face", to help others, and enable him to have a fresh career. To God be the glory!

"Cast all your anxiety on him because he cares for you"
1 Peter 5:7

42. Revisiting the edge – with great care.
Eleanor's story.

Eleanor had enrolled on a Listening Post Introductory Course. She had good intelligence and seemed keen and capable. However it was not long before she found herself doubting the wisdom of continuing with the full course and sought our counselling help. One of the Supervisors on the Training Team had observed that Eleanor seemed to be worried about parts of the course. I do not know what or who prompted her to seek counselling, but when the supervisor (lets call her "Jane") sat down with her, Eleanor showed that she was troubled by complicated mental processes. Jane asked if I could join the sessions so that together we might be able to help Eleanor find answers. She had seen and heard me leading the course and explaining what Christian Counselling was all about. It was helpful that she had sat through the parts of the Introductory Course about listening skills, a non-judgemental attitude, enabling to gently help troubled people tell their story their way. As we stressed confidentiality and providing a safe place this must have struck a chord with her. Both Jane and I assessed that she was well motivated, intelligent, yet was clearly showing signs of inner confusion. We decided that we must take our time enabling her to feel sufficiently confident in us to reveal what was going on inside. So we asked her permission to pray simply with her, and then prayed earnestly for wisdom.

So it was that we met over several months. This is how she recalled those sessions some 16 years later as she wrote the following account to be used in this book –*"One of the most important aspects of being counselled is the 'safe place'. If trusting people has been a difficult issue in life, then the idea of safety is vitally important. As I began being counselled with Listening Post I was asked to draw my safe place. I actually drew a complex pattern of overhead leaves and tree trunks; as though I was in a wood, surrounded by trees in leaf looking up to the sky through a circle of overhanging branches. It did not much physically resemble the little room where I could share my inside story, but the two people who sat patiently week after week gave me an equally safe place, quiet, undisturbed, not overlooked and, in it's way, beautiful. I knew that DW was always praying for me during these sessions. My faith was not very big. so I always hoped that I would not be asked to pray. I was so grateful that prayer was covering the whole process. I felt like a part Christian. Something was very confused inside, and I was troubled by the "darkness" in my spirit which I could not get rid of. I was terrified by being touched, but as I knelt down on the floor with my counsellor, probably doing some drawing, I remember my hair brushing against hers– and it was OK. More than that, it was connection and I had survived. I found it difficult to trust, but trust started to grow. Together we gradually explored different parts of my rather complex personality, which had become shattered, but for which I had no explanation. Never feeling like a complete person, changing from adult to child, having strong attachments and strong aversions sometimes to the same person, sometimes feeling numb and remote and totally unable to connect. I had a responsible job which I managed pretty well. I was a wife and a mother to three student-aged children. I functioned, but inside was chaotic, especially spiritually.*

David:

It was a privilege to have such important feed-back. I had a very unusual role literally being primarily a praying presence in the room, holding the boundaries of what she aptly called her "safe place". Without that she would never have gone home and written a list of the nine characters into whose personae she had taken refuge. That allowed Jane to meet each of those individually, to talk with them through you, to sit or play on the floor with them, and draw.... Being there with them both was my great privilege – and then to pray that Eleanor would never again need to hide in fear.

At the close of each time together I prayed aloud, that Eleanor would feel the Love of Jesus within and around, and find the wholeness of the Eleanor whom God had created. As in turn we met all nine of her intimate friends Eleanor emerged complete and whole... gradually. She wrote:

The patient unconditional love I experienced whilst being coun-selled began to teach me about God's Love. I am amazed that folk would sit with me hour after hour and listen, and be there for me. At the time I did not realise as much as I do now, but the commitment to work alongside someone like I was, is won-derful, and can only be an expression of His Love.

David:

I had learnt about "Dissociative Identity Disorder", "DID", the study of which was new in the counselling world. There was a group in ACC which was subsequently called "TAG" "Survivors of Trauma and Abuse Group" – and Mike Fisher (who was a founder of Willows in Swindon – a contemporary of mine) was also a founder member of TAG. [82] Basically, a person who has experienced traumatic or abusive treatment learns to take refuge in the altered personality of another. At that time the "alter" is real to them. They become that person. That is how we met each of Eleanor's "inside people" until she became safe and whole – and did not need to take refuge. We never did know the circumstances which triggered what to many would seem bizarre revelations. But we had living proof of John's proclama-tion that "Perfect love drives out fear" (1 John 4:18) Hers was a very deep-seated fear…. The healing process was not com-plete when we parted. She was functioning so much better, and we encouraged Eleanor to find nurture with the skilled Pastoral Team in Eleanor's church. Jane and I met with their leader to facilitate this. This was another example of "**Together**". We, in effect, handed over the baton to them.

My counsellors changed. Different people for different sea-sons. I had invaluable help from my church. Much later I was to learn how many people were called upon to support the lady who counselled me in prayer. Is it any wonder I am now so changed? For ten years she has "been there" for me. I have had to be weaned off over-dependency, a huge danger and not an unexpected one. Interestingly God could use my counsel-lor's illness to ensure that the dependency ceased! Praying into the situations which I could not remember brought pictures and events to mind of which I knew nothing. But I was able to visualise Jesus there sometimes. At other times he simply took away any feelings, or gave me reassurance. Because I always want everything to make sense logically, he also enabled this to happen. I would begin to trace patterns in events and see connections, and this made it easier for me. Living out the rest of my life was difficult. With the increased counselling I was for some time more aware of "changing"or "switching" from one personality to another, and would be really afraid I would stick and not be able to return to pick up the rest of my life. Gradually I could identify triggers which would cause me to switch. As each personality began to speak within the counselling situation there was a great sense of relief and freedom which was wonderful. But so often I would feel that it was not real and I'd be hounded by guilt that I was making it all up, This I understand to be quite normal in the circumstances. I could not always remember what went on within the counselling sessions. I was always very grateful to have time to return to the "core" me, to make it to the car, and get safely home. The question of sufficient time is a difficult one for that reason .It is extremely hard for someone who has DID to function if they leave counselling in an altered state. There is much confusion and risk attached to that situation. One by one the different parts of my personality were integrated, or in some instance was not needed, and allowed to go. This always felt strange and frightening, but actually **it is OK !** Once they have done their job they are free to go.

Mine has been a long journey, but that is probably par for the course. God is faithful. He has worked through a variety of people in differing counselling situations. I am amazed at His patience as demonstrated in those who sought to help me. Knowing they were there for me, eventually led me to realise that He was there for me. As I became much more whole, much more confident and less afraid of people, I felt I wanted to embark on some Bible study course, to ground myself in this still fragile faith. I was introduced to inductive Bible study, and once again God provided just the right step next. Through spending more time in the Word my faith is developing. I have still a long way to go, but the road is clearer, my resolve is greater, and my vision clearer.

*Healing has undoubtedly taken place. God hasn't finished with me but I press on…. Knowing **He is the enabler.***

"But thanks be to God who always leads us in triumphal procession in Christ and through us spreads everywhere the fragrance of the knowledge of him."
2 Corinthians 2:14

Part Five

SO WHAT?

42. "Meanwhile back at the ranch"

As we began with "little boy dddavid" I am ending on a personal note. I would never have written this book if several people had not enquired when I was going to write my memoires. The chief prompter was Tracey, my daughter-in-law. Some people frankly have thought me a bit mad, being so single-minded in life about working with delinquents or people who have difficulties. Others have just been curious about why people like me bother with "crooks" or mentally abnormal people.

I firmly believe that they are just mortals like you and me, some of whom have acted in a crooked way. Secretly, others may have been critical that my family seemed to take second place. Frankly there was some truth in that accusation, but it did challenge me to try to multi-task and prioritize. Nevertheless, sometimes there have been conflicts for which there seemed to be no easy solution. Thanks to Mary always holding the home base, and being sacrificial in her caring, we have got by. Even when I was commuting on five different vehicles per day each way across the sea to prison on the Isle of Wight!

I became very enthusiastic for Christian caring organisations such as "Care for the Family"[87] who crossed denominational boundaries. My colleagues showed the way with caring. They especially befriended Mary, and on one memorable occasion the group of Supervisors in Listening Post ganged up on me and (kindly) told me to take a month out. I had not realised just how tired I was, but they "cared enough to confront" me. I needed them to rebel. Immediately I obediently stopped working I felt great relief. It was then that I bought Edward England's "The Addiction of a busy Life". [85] Rob Parsons of "Care for the Family" said in the Foreword that this book could help many who lived well-meaning lives. Hopefully we will not all need a heart attack like Edward. But within a month I relaxed, lost concentration whilst driving, and wrote off my car! It was very salutary!

That wake-up call was necessary! I reviewed that book grate-fully in ACCord. Edward England had written: "This book could save your life". Certainly I tried to take his lessons to heart, but in such things I am a slow learner!

In February 1999 I met Gary Collins of USA Association of Christian Counsellors, and interviewed him for "ACCord". He had just published "Breathless" [86] and as I read that book later I realised that the lessons in it about living a more balanced life were really for me too. I liked his Chapter 8 particularly – "Sharing and growing together". He says that geese fly in a V formation and thereby get 71% greater range together than by flying alone. They also look after their wounded en route. This was in a section on Teamwork, and working together in a focussed way. The Listening Post team looked after Mary, and ensured that she was in social events, and at seminars espe-cially. That way she felt part of the team. Though she was not a counsellor she did reception work well, and was involved in the Cheltenham branch. Gary Collins urged his readers to "Care for the Family"[87], and the UK organisation by that name does some of the best Christian caring work, with Pregnancy Crisis Centres, and teaching tours such as "Praying home the Prodigals".

In Probation days I saw many broken families, victims of abuse, domestic violence, addictions. I shuddered when pae-dophiles were released into their home communities. Probation services helped start Victim Support Schemes. We prepared reports on custody of divorced children and access to sepa-rated parents; and witnessed much serious neglect. However, I was conscious that at times my own children did not get the attention which I commended to parents. I am still a supporter and admirer of "Care for the family" and commend them for their educational and campaigning roles. That seemed hypocritical – and troubled me. Nevertheless my children did more than just survive, and I am proud of them both – and my two talented granddaughters. I want to pause briefly to tell you about them.

Teresa was born in 1963 when we lived in Epsom and I worked at Sainsburys. My promotion meant that we moved to a village near Basingstoke. This was seemingly idyllic. We were relatively well off. Settled into the village community, with lovely neighbours and many young friends. Mary and her friend started the village Young wives Club and I started a youth club. Then that 4am call made us make dramatic changes – to less money, many more moves…Thenceforward, the family went through several upheavals. Teresa was good at making friends, and still has contact with friends from her past home areas.

Mary too made her closest friend there, and this friend-ship supported her through the times of my Probation Training. Stephen was born in 1965, and then the family had the first major change. Mary was the one who had difficulties coping with leaving her supportive community of friends just as she needed them most. Hers was the greatest sacrifice – but she never complained – and always encouraged me. This was when I learnt to compartmentalise my life. I could not share at home the tests and excitements of my new job – especially the juicy but confidential bits. I had to tune in at home. The struggle was to not treat my family as second best. I was thrilled to see Teresa walk, then Stephen play, and watch both enjoying their friends… My parents retired near our home in Kingsclere. There we saw the Queen's horses trained – and my mother captured them in water colour – and got commended for it by the Royal trainer! My Dad wrote his book in his new cottage study! (Their first home that they owned!) We enjoyed village life, Wives Group, Youth Club, friendly church, a higher salary… It seemed even more idyllic! Then I seemingly wrecked it by working away a lot and changing jobs and moving!!!!. It was all confusing for the children. So we moved into new worlds in Fareham, Hampshire, where both children started School and sought to find new friends. Mary once again was helping the children cope with the changes when she was least able to adjust herself.

As I recall those days I am increasingly conscious of another irony. In my subsequent professions I continuously tried to help people to change their ways of life, and to cope with changes and events which throw them off balance. On several occasions I made my own family cope with confusing changes, and it is scarcely surprising that they were at times left feeling resentful when things went off balance in our own lives.

So I do hope that this book may go just a little way to help them understand what was going on in my life which I could never describe to them. More importantly I hope they will begin to see how sad it makes me feel that my concentration on the needs of others made them sometimes seem to be pushed into my background.

Meantime, back at the ranch...

Our numerous family photo albums remind us of really happy times as a family especially when we teamed up with Adrian (Whom I have nick-named "Mr. Serendipity" earlier) and Katherine Stanley. They had children exactly the same age and sex as ours, and this developed into a close friendship of our two families. We shared so much fun, most holidays, and most values. Even now, it would seem a strange Christmas if we did not share it. Rosamund Stanley did a Librarian degree, and Teresa trained as a teacher. Mark eventually followed his father into work with offenders - and most recently Rosamund has worked in the Administrative team in Cheltenham where her late father was Senior Probation Officer.

I have been thrilled to see Teresa relish her work as an Infant teacher in Bristol which she has enjoyed for more than twenty years. Her imaginative way of enabling young children lay sound educational foundations has gained her recent pro-motion and enabled her to express her talents through supervi-sion and liaison with parents. In common with me, Teresa never wanted to give up the hands on experience in which she excels. Her husband Steve, who works in the Ministry of Defence, has learnt new skills in catering for the two girls to allow Teresa cope with the new responsibilities and time-consuming supervision and extra-mural work. It has been a great pleasure for us to see their two daughters grow up so well with different talents. Bethany (13) is very extravert and good at games. especially swimming. She has an excellent sense of humour and lots of friends. Jennifer (now 18) is very talented in performing arts, singing, dancing and drama.

Sadly, she went through a stage of being seriously bullied, but we were really glad when some girls at school befriended her. They introduced her to their Baptist Youth Club, where she found a new interest. "Jenny" was inspired by "Soul Survivor" meetings.

Nevertheless, circumstances have meant that we have seen more of Stephen in recent years, because he and I shared interests in walking and the countryside. We both love dogs and wild-life. He and I have had several exciting walking holidays together, walking the South Downs Way, the Pennine Way, and in the Lake District. I thought of those walks as I described "Counselling on the Edge" .Mounting Scafell Pike up a dried stream, or Helvellyn up Striding Edge with challenging dangers rewarded by magnificent vistas seems to symbolise the joys of shared achievement. When he was seventeen, "Steve" had rather resented having to move to Gloucester from Hampshire, where he had many friends.

He had wanted to be a farmer, but found himself working at Sainsburys, the grocery firm where I used to work. This gave him some good friends, but no prospects of promotion. Fortunately, Mary spotted an advert for work at the Government Communications Headquarters in Cheltenham. After six months of vetting and selection, Steve was chosen to work there. That ends what I know and can record, but friends he gained there spoke well about his work. One of the people in the same office was an ex RAF man called Martin. They became friendly, and quite close when Martin developed virulent skin cancer, which led to Martin's eventual medical retirement. Steve met Tracey, Martin's wife (who also worked at GCHQ) and eventually he introduced Martin to us. Over the next two years we shared important times with Tracey and Martin, and liked their company. I admired Martin, who was a brave, intelligent, caring man.

Steve loves deer, and he did have a standing photographic exhibition for three years at Chedworth Roman Villa Nature Reserve, and his best photos featured deer. He also went on some adventure holidays in mountains, then two wonderful African Safaris. It was in Namibia and Botswana that his life changed dramatically. Whilst in an encampment, Steve slept in a tent on his own. In the dead of night someone entered his tent. Steve awoke to feel breeze from the tent flap, and horror of horrors, £2000 worth of photographic equipment and 16 completed rolls of film GONE! The shock of this was so great that it triggered neurological balance problems which developed into a most debilitating stutter. Though he does not recollect any injury to his head, later tests revealed damage to his cerebellum. Suffice it to say that over the next four years, Steve became progressively less able to carry out his work at GCHQ. Extensive tests at Frenchay Neurological Unit led eventually to medical retirement. He had been quite happy and successful in the Government job. So this was a big change for him.

During this period, sadly Steve's close friend Martin died after many operations and much other treatment. He was courageous to the end, often cycling some 14 miles a day just to prove that the illness had not beaten him. I was privileged to be one of a team who watched at his bedside during his last two weeks – and to pray with him. It was a privilege to know this brave man – and his lovely wife, Tracey! It seemed as if they were in our family – and they soon were!

A year later (3 October 2009), Steve and Tracey were married. It was a lovely occasion Our two granddaughters were beautiful bridesmaids. We were so glad that they eventually moved to a lovely new home in the Forest of Dean. This 15 miles from our home and is adjacent to the well-known Wilderness Nature Reserve Steve and Tracey has five acres of land with deer nearby, and a 200 year old cottage which is being renovated to become a workshop for Steve. Their two Border collie dogs seem to think this is seventh heaven.

I tell this story in some detail, because I think it is no coincidence that the shock from Steve's injuries have resulted in a "neurological stutter". This is very different from my stutter, but both were triggered by post-traumatic stress. However I do pray that he may be helped by my empathy and by my faith during whatever years we can share together. Certainly, Mary and I plan to see our family much more frequently during whatever years we are granted of retirement together.

So this is a story of wonderful family, friends, and travelling companions on the journeys of life. God did carry us through stormy seas, beyond the difficulties, so that we sought to follow His way – TOGETHER. "And it was good!"

On 1 December 2000 we held a Celebration Service for all that had passed in Listening Post and prayed for all that was to come. I am left with so many happy memories and each time I turn through the pages of names, I am filled with deep emotion, mainly of gratitude for shared adventure with the Lord – sometimes into very new territory. That is why I wanted to write this book – to recall some of the miracles of healing, and the opportunities of cross fertilisation of faith experience, which enabled such different people moulded into a team which gave many hurting people chances to realistically seek and find listening ears, and new hope of peace and wholeness - often in place of fear and despair.

So we recall changed lives, hundreds of them. During ten years we trained well over 200 Christians in Gloucestershire to be competent counsellors in a service which was among the pioneer organisations of this new profession. It was always a steep learning curve. We sought to learn from people nationally who were of like mind. Together we sought to improve the quality of our training standards and service. We grew through making links in the national Christian and secular educational and counselling systems. For example, we linked with local colleges, including Redcliffe Bible College. We reached out to many local community groups. Some of our counsellors moved away and joined other counselling and healing services. Our Training course was taken to nearby Worcester to start a similar service, called "The Bridge", there. So the time came for me to retire from being Director of Listening Post, and I knew it was time to "Let go and Let God" guide them on.

I was very pleased when my successor was Sheila Appleton, an oblate of the Convent at Wantage, whence Sister Margaret Magdalen came. It was a wonderful heritage. Sheila had worked with us previously as a Supervisor, and had also led a mental health charity. She was better equipped than me to link up with the local medical profession. After discussions, and much prayer, I decided to make a complete break to allow them to follow the route that God would lead them on the next phase. It would be different. But I must trust God to guide them on. It was not easy to let go of "my baby". I decided to trust them to continue to let God guide them. They continued to develop and to be more recognised as a relevant Christian community caring resource. For that I thank God.

So I learnt to play saxophone and clarinet, played in a small praise band and 30 piece "Jazz 2 Go" 30 piece band eventually. That kept my brain stretched (Thank you Kath Baker, my patient teacher!). I did more gardening and walking.... And praying.

A Postscript.

Counsellors often say that, as the client goes out the door, he or she says "Oh! I forgot to tell you..." This is a sort of Postscript like that. I nearly forgot to write about the rude awakening I had in 2002! "I must just tell you –"and it IS relevant to the theme."

In 2002 I went to a meeting of 100 men in Lonsdale Road Methodist Church. Most of us really did not want to be there. A specialist was talking about Prostate Cancer, and Chris Gibbs, a Methodist Minister came right out saying **"I've got TERMINAL Prostate Cancer** and if you have these symptoms see about it **NOW"**.

Well, I had, and I did, and I thank Chris for his witness, and the three specialists who saw to me over the next two years. Yes, it was a shock – and I was soon in hospital twice, and had 30 doses of radiotherapy, and hormone therapy (conning my body I was female and therefore not supposed to have pros-tate cancer!). But here I am able to tell the tale. It was inconvenient. I had arranged to lead a whole day's seminar on "Anger and Conflict Resolution" at Harnhill Healing Centre. So I worked hard on it, too hard! Suffice it to say, I should not have continued. My old pride got in the way, and I did a less than good job with a very important subject. "Pride comes before a fall" AGAIN!. My only compensation was that the excessively huge wad of handouts I produced were well received and might just have informed a few people about relevant literature…It did show me how crisis can shake anyone – but God does pick us up and carry us through and beyond it.

I was one of at least four people who were able to thank Chris for his witness before he did die. Eight years later I still have check-ups, but I am really grateful for the skill of medical staff. A few years on I suddenly started seeing double, and found that I had a haemorrhage behind an eye. My blood pressure was almost off the scale. A skilled optometrist covered the eye and said that x-rays did not reveal a blood vessel there - "but there might be one!" Well there was, and my sight was restored in that eye in three months! WOW!

I do thank God for answers to prayer and His healing mercy which has allowed this book to be written. There is so much more I could have written about the hundreds of lovely people who have walked beside me on this journey. They are all very special people – and precious in His sight. It has been a privilege to live, love, learn and grow in His service,

together.

43, In Conclusion.
Learning to Listen by Listening to Learn, TOGETHER.

Togetherness is not always easy, but it is best.

When the seas of life are rough, then travelling with God does carry us through and beyond the difficulties. When we met people who seemed to be seriously travelling "On the Edge" of life, then we discovered with them the power in their single-minded motivation to be persistent in asking prayerfully to be shown the way. The nine true stories entitled "Counselling on the edge" all have this in common. These lovely individuals were very different. God heard their prayers, and healed them. I thank them for sharing their stories, generously offered as each person wanted to express their gratitude to our Wonderful Counsellor who demonstrated the miracles of His Healing Grace. This is the testimony to the distinctiveness of Christian Counselling.

It was when I reached out in tearful desperation in that telephone box out outside LSE that my journey of discovery began. It slowly dawned on me that He had heard my cries of desperation. Just as asuffering woman in the crowd around Jesus had plucked up the courage to reach out to touch him, he had felt that touch, heard her plea, and focussed all of his healing power onto her. Our experience through "Counselling on the edge" was that the healing Love of Jesus consistently came true in the lives of hurting people today when we learned to listen, trust and seek to act, empowered by the love of Jesus within.. Matthew recalled that Jesus amazingly promised in his Sermon on the Mount: "Ask and it will be given" (Matthew 7:7). He did not say it would always be given instantaneously, and in the disciples' journeys with Jesus they learnt just how painful was the journey. Nevertheless, it was in the Upper Room, on the Emmaus Road, and on the shores of Galilee that they all learned how Jesus cared enough to confront Peter, and transformed him so he could become the Rock on which his church could be founded. In 1754 John Newton, the repentant slave trader discovered the power in the forgiveness that Jesus gave to those who crucified him. He repented, and wonderfully witnessed to freedom through forgiveness in one of the best known hymns: "Amazing Grace." Joanne (Chapter 36) tells us how she found healing and peace from vengeful passions, and that forgiving love was not only possible but enabled her to find new freedom.[75] My father in his book stressed the importance of Transforming Love in healing. I know that his handling of my growing up problems showed me loving boundaries and "tough Love" – backed by single-minded prayer. His allowing me to play with him, then obediently sending us across the Atlantic, was a frightening test of Faith and Love. I thank God for loving relatives in USA and UK, whose witness enriched my life then – and now.

In Listening Post we found continually that prayer-soaked counselling was empowered by the Holy Spirit, just as the Apostles had learnt in the early church, I claim that this was why transformations occurred with each of the people quoted in "Counselling on the Edge". Their witness confirms that.

In 1993 Father Gerard Hughes wrote his "Journey through Lent for bruised pilgrims." He presented many questions such as "O God Why?" [88] In writing my book I have just wanted to celebrate the journeys of the many pilgrims I met and with whom I have travelled. I wanted to pay special tribute to the pioneers of Christian Counselling. The bibliography (or "Endnotes" as Americans call them) lists the works of many wise people who have contributed so much to the sum total of knowledge of the topography of our Way. It is their diversity and their strength which is summed up in Selwyn Hughes' wonderful "Everyday with Jesus" Bible Reading Notes for Nov/Dec 2005 "Strong in the broken places" [89] written just before his death in January 2006. That edition celebrates God's promise that "my power is made perfect in weakness" [90] It is a tribute that these notes still inspire millions five years since his death, because the scriptural truths which he proclaimed never change. The woven cord on the cover symbolises strength through adversity, and diversity. Two of the pioneers of Christian Counselling (Mike Sheldon and Dave Ames) chose the title for their foundational book, "To bind up the broken hearted" [91]

I have no doubt that much of the counselling we did in Probation was helpful, and people did find ways to change. However, it was when we allowed the "Wonderful Counsellor" to guide our work, then amazing things happened.. Denominational differences and childish fears melted into insignificance as we worked together single-mindedly.

God does not take our dark times away, but he does promise to carry us through and beyond them. Just as Jesus set his face to go to Jerusalem and his cross, so his Love empowers us to face our situations in His strength.

Reach out, trust him, and claim his promised Legacy of Peace.(John 16:33)

"My Peace I leave with you".

Appendix One

S ome details of the progress of Counselling Training during the initial ten years of Listening Post Christian Counselling Service.

1990/1   Introductory Courses at Gloucester Royal Hospital School of Midwifery
             Over 70 people attended in total, of whom 44 went onto

1992/3   One Year Course based on Network's course.
             Listening Post opened in Gloucester June 1991 with 34 counsellors who all required further training – partially through weekend seminars.

1993/4   One Year Course at St. Pauls School of Midwifery, Cheltenham
             54 completed this course. Cheltenham branch opened Dec with 26 counsellors

             New ACC criteria –Introductory and Foundation Course 50 hours
             Pre-Accreditation 200 hours Fee £200

1995/7   New Combined Course at Stroud Baptist Church.
             Stroud opened Sept 1997.

1997   Liaison discussions with Open College Network/ Bilston Community College

            Future courses approved by Open College Network

1997/9   Introductory and Foundation Course with Pre-Accreditation held with sessions at Redcliffe College, Cheltenham and Tewkesbury

270774   Open College- approved Marriage Counselling Course

1999/2000   Gloscat became more involved.

270775   Listening Post Trainers Sarah and Neil Jones took Listening Post courses to Worcester. This enabled The Bridge at Worcester to be formed, with former Listening Post Counsellor, Sue Cockeram as Director.

            Sarah and Neil Jones then counselled with Barnabas Trust and Gloucester Diocesan Counselling Service

            In total more than 240 Christians have completed our "Main Courses" which after 1995 were Two year Courses. We were always seeking to improve standards and valued the help and guidance of ACC, The Open College Network and Gloucester College of Art and technology ("GLOSCAT")

Listening Post Training Seminar Programme

Listening Post held a series of Saturday Seminars to supplement our Training Courses.

These cost £10 per day and average attendance was 40 – 60

Dates	Titles	Speakers
5/92	Gifts of the Spirit in Counselling	Sheila Smith
9/91	Marriage Counselling	David and Christine Mitchell of Network, Bristol
10/91	The Fair face of Evil	Nigel Wright
11/91	Learning to Love	True Freedom Trust
2/92	Child Abuse	Georgina Robinson – Social Services
3/92	Aids and HIV	Dr. David Maxted, GP Hucvclecote, Gloucester
10/92	Drug Abuse	Stuart Waddington, Coke hole Trust, Andover
11/92	Groupwork	David Walker
12/92	Sexual Problems	Margaret Gill
2/93	Healing Dreams	Rev. Russ Parker, Acorn Healing Trust
3/93	Eating Disorders	Dr. Jill Welbourne Bristol Royal Infirmary
9/93	Guilt and forgiveness	Rev Dorothy Knowles
10/93	Myers Briggs Personality Inventory,	Grace Ministries
1/94	Prayer Counselling	Rev Peter Nash
2/94	Rejection	Stephen Hepden, Ellel Grange

3/94	Facing Death	Dr. Averil Stedeford, formerly Sobell House, Oxford
5/94	Alternative therapies	Doug Harris, Reach Out Trust
6/94	Domestic Violence	Julia Conway, Listening Post
9/94	Family Therapy	Dr. E A Guinness
11/94	Marriage Counselling	David Walker and Nan Willson, Listening Post
2/95	Children and adolescents	Karen Mitchell and Diane Rowe
3/95	Creativity in Counselling	Rev W. Denning
7/95	Anger Management Part One	David Walker and Julia Conway L.P.
9/95	Addiction Release	Pat Prosser, Life for the World Trust
12/95	Psychiatry and the Holy Spirit	Dr. Roger Moss
2/96	A Christian approach to Neuro linguistic Programming	Neil Jones
5/96	Bereavement Care	Rev. Graham Jones (Cheltenham)
9/96	Counselling and Sex Offenders	Malcolm Worsley, Phillipi Trust, Blackpool
10/96	Post Abortion Counselling	Joanna Thompson, Care for the Family
4/97	Holistic Mental Health	Sheila Appleton, Mind
5/97	Transactional Analysis	Christine Jones-Wood of St Johns, Nottingham
6/97	Anger Management, Part Two	Brian Jones, David Walker, Julia Dean
1/98	Creative Techniques in Christian Counselling	Mary Strachan CC International

2/98	Eating Disorders	Helena Wilkinson
3/98	Stress Counselling	Wanda Nash, UK international Stress Management Assoc
11/98	A Christian view of Homosexuality	Maranatha Ministries
1/99	Trauma, Putting the pieces together	K. Cairns.

Appendix Two
ACC – our "catalyst for excellence" - hot issues
in Accord 2000 – 2011

The voice of Christian Counselling – Sean Gubb, Chair of ACC	Spring 2002
The dark side of Family - Gary Haire	Autumn 2002
Peacemaking, a Biblical Perspective, Philip Greenslade	Winter 2003
The value of books – Joe Story and David Depledge	Autumn 2004
Culture and its implications for Christian Counselling, Dr. Rhoda Paul	Autumn 2004
Crossing the cultural divide, Judith Bradley,, ex Nepal, and CWR	Winter 2004
Into all the world, and Cyberspace by John Court	Spring 2006

The impact of social disadvantage and marginalisation in counselling process and relationship, Barbra Depledge, Coventry — Autumn 2006

Committed to excellence by Syd Platt — Autumn 2006

The Secret Sin by Tony Tufnell — Winter 2006

CBT and Religious Activity, Rob Waller, Consultant Psychiatrist — Spring 2007

Cognitive Behaviour Therapy Excellent series by Paul Hepplethwaite Regulation – Rhetoric or Reality? Great Randle and John Nightingale — Autumn 2008

(Most editions have update articles on this saga from David Depledge) — Summer 2002

Pastoral Care: The challenge of difference, Teresa Onions — Summer 2008

Focussing and Experimental Psychotherapy by John Threadgold — Autumn 2008

The Glory of Christian Counselling and Psychotherapy. Dr. Eric L. Johnson Kentucky USA — Spring 2009

Seeking to bring peace to the trauma of ritual abuse Mike Fisher Chair of TAG Articles in Spring 2002, Winter 2003, Beyond disbelief — Spring 2009

Endnotes and Bibliography

Preface

1. Through all the changing scenes of life by Nahum Tate and Nicholas Brady – (Based on Psalm 34) Hymns and Psalms Methodist Publishing House 1983
2. God of Surprises by Gerard W. Hughes Pub. Darton, Longman and Todd, 1985
3. John Wesley's Sermons. "The Almost Christian"
4. St. Paul's Damascus Road Conversion Acts 9. NIV
5. Love is a choice by Robert Hemfelt, Frank Minirth, Paul Meier Pub. By Thomas Nelson 1989
6. The Hidden Face of Jesus by Margaret Magdalen CSMV Pub Darton, Longman and Todd, London 1994
7. Roots and Shoots. A Guide to Counselling and Psychotherapy by Roger Hurding. Pub. Hodder and Stoughton 1985
8. Christian Counselling. A Comprehensive Guide by Gary Collins 1988
Pub Thomas Nelson, USA
9. The Counselling of Jesus by Duncan Buchanan. Pub by Hodder, 1985
10. The Purpose-driven Life by Rick Warren Pub. By Zondervan 2002

Part One. Through and Beyond stormy seas

11. "He's still workin' on me" by Joel Hemphill, in "Great is the Lord" Songs arranged by Tom Fette 1984 Lillenas Publishing Co. Kansas 64141

12. Crisis Intervention: Selected Readings – Howard J. Parad, Editor. Family Service Association of America, NY 10010 1965

13. Boundaries by Dr. Henry Cloud and Dr. John Townsend A classic series of over 27 books published by Zondervan from 1992

14. Ecclesiastes 3:11 NIV "He has made everything beautiful in its time" NIV

15. There but for the Grace of God Go I" the 16th century English evangelist and martyr is remembered as saying when he saw many criminals burnt at the stake. He is remembered by 1000 pages of writings. "None of us have the right to claim that we are not capable of sin."

16. Pompey's Gentleman Jim – Peter Jeffs - Breedon Books Sport 45 Friar Gate, Derby, DE1 1DA. Biography of Jimmy Dickenson MBE .

17. History of the London School of Economics and Political Science 1895-1995
Ralf Dahrendorf Open University Press Oxford UK 1995.
It was in this magnificent Library that I devoured many books which taught
foundations for me on Psychology, sociology and criminology.

18. "Ephphatha" Mark 7:31-37 NIV describes the healing of the deaf mute to whose distress Jesus responded with "Open up" – and he was healed. "Jesus commanded the people to tell no one. They were overwhelmed with amazement 'He has done everything well' they said. 'He even makes the deaf hear and the mute speak'

19. Asking. In teaching his followers to pray Jesus says. "Your Father knows what you need before you ask Him" (Matthew 6:8) but He still teaches us to "Ask, and it will be given to you, knock and the door will be opened to you" (Mt 7:7-12)

20. When the needy woman bravely reached out in pain, Jesus responded with compassion and she was healed. (Matthew 9:21) NIV

21. "I the Lord of Seas and Sky...... I heard you calling in the night" 830 in Songs of Fellowship published by Kingsway Music2003

22. "Miss Potter" DVD Momentum Pictures starring Rene Zellweger & Ewan McGregor

Part Two On Probation

23. Changing Lives An oral history of Probation. Published in 2007 by NAPO
The Trade Union and professional association for Probation staff.

24. Casework in Probation by Mark Monger, MA. Senior Lecturer, School of Social Work University of Leicester. Published by Butterworths 1972,

25. Crisis Intervention: Ed H Parad (Family Association of Amrica 1965) is referred to by Monger (above) Pages 25 onwards commenting on the family crises of Court appearance, Fear of the outcome affects motivation to change.

26. Sense and Nonsense in Psychology by H. J. Eysenck Pelican 1957was one of
many popularised books on Psychology

27. Emotional Problems of Living, by O. Spurgeon English and Gerald H J Pearson
Allen & Unwin 1947/63."Avoiding the neurotic pattern" A standard textbook
on the Home Office Course led by Herschel Prins.

28. Offenders, Deviants, or Patients? An introduction to the study of socio-forensic
problems by Herschel Prins, Tavistock Publications 1980

29. The Alpha Drug Unit in Hampshire gained a reputation for its behaviourist treatment methods developed the theory that some recidivist criminals were equally addicted to crime.

30. The Mission to Marriage Course was led by Dave and Joyce Ames at Lee Abbey, N. Devon England which Mary and I benefited from in 1993.
The Stress-free Marriage – published by CrossWay Books, Eastbourne, 1990.
Dave Ames was a Board Member of Assoc. of Christian Counsellors.

31. "He's still workin' on me, to make me what I oughta be" from collection of songs arranged by Tom Fette, pub. by Lillenas in Kansas, USA – "Great is the Lord"

32. Psalm 86:11 "Teach me your Way.O Lord, Help me to walk in your Truth" NIV

33. The Church of Judas by J. Hollis Walker; Published 1968 by Muriel Walker
Printed by Epworth Press. "Hollis Walker passed into the Fuller Life on 4th March 1968 before arrangements for publication could be completed."

34. Facing Death by Averil Stedeford, MRC Psych Dept of Psychotherapy
Warnford Hospital, Oxford, England, and Sir Michael Sobell House, Oxford
William Heinemann Medical Books Ltd, London.

35. Love is a Choice – Dr. R Hemfelt, Dr F. Minirth, Dr. P Meier
Published by Thomas Nelson, Nashville 1989

36 Accenchuate the Positive = song by Johnny Mercer. Written 1943
The story of his life has a chapter on this song – "SkylarK" Philip Furia, St. Martins Press NY 2003. Song published by Mercer's Capitol Records.

37. Caring enough to confront, and Caring enough to forgive. byDavid Augsberger Published by Regal Books,California, USA 1981

38. The Serenity Prayer – used by Alcoholics Anonymous to close their meetings.
"God grant me the serenity to accept the things I cannot change, the courage to change the things I can, and the wisdom to know the difference."

39. Shared Phantasy in Marital Problems. Therapy in a four-person Relationship by Kathleen Bannister and Lily Pincus, Institute of Marital Studies, Tavistock Institute of Human Relations 1965

40. The Twisting Lane by Tony Parker, Panther modern Society 1969

41. "Rule 43" is the Prison Rule under which a prisoner who considers him/herself under threat can apply for segregation for protection.

42. "Porridge" series of TV comedy films starring Ronnie Barker on prison life.

43. Hansard Report of the Written and oral evidence of BASW Treatment of Offenders', 15th Report of the House of Commons Expenditure Committee

44. NACRO News – "Inside Out" Article by David Walker on 1977 placement with Ohio State Probation Service experiencing "Shock Probation", combining 66 county services into one state service.

45. Carl Rogers, the founder of Client-centred Therapy – On Becoming a Person Constable 1967. CR Rogers "A Way of Being" 1980, Boston, Houghton Mifflin; Brian Thorne "Person-centred Counselling: Therapeutic and Spiritual Dimensions Pub. Whurr London1991

46. Adrian Stanley's article Justice of Peace article 17 Sept 1977, reproduced in Prison Services Journal on "Care Control and Punishment".

47. Adrian Stanley briefly quoted in Foren and Bailey's "Authority in Social Casework" 1968 Pergamon Press.

48. Prison Over-crowding campaigns by NACRO. Eg. Article in their Newsletter "Insight". Show that UK Prison Population doubled from 44, 553 in 1993 to 85.000 in 2010

49. Community Development and Crime – by David Walker Social Work Today Vol 8 no33 24 May 1977 Article on Leigh Park, Havant Hants, UK "Off the Record" was opened a year after this article was published.

50. The Second Mile by Roger Grainger,50 years 1938-2008Langley House Trust.

Part 3 Towards a Christian Counselling Service

51. See colour pages on the pioneer work of the Association of Christian Counsellors and organisations like Network, Manna, Lighthouse, Listening Post, Willows, Barnabas, Cardiff Concern, etc, etc. etc.

55. Restoring the Image by Roger Hurding, 1980 Paternoster Press
An introduction to Christian Counselling
Roots and Shoots by Roger Hurding, 1985 Hodder & Stoughton
A guide to counselling and psychotherapy.

56. Testing the waters

57. Clinical Psychology by Frank Lake

58. Psalm 86:11 NIV

59. Christian Counselling by Gary Collins, 1988 Pub. Thomas Nelson (Revised Edn)

60. The use of Psalms for spiritual and emotional growth by David J. Bick,
Pub Excalibur Press of London, 1992

61. Finding a way out 1 Cor. 10:13

62. Competent to Counsel by Jay E. Adams, Pub Baker 1970
The foundation book of Nouthetic Biblical Counselling

63. Listening Post's Statement of Aims

64. Paul planted in Corinth, and Apollos watered Acts 18;24-28, 1 Cor. 3:6&7.

65. God of Surprises by Gerard W Hughes 1985 Darton, Longman and Todd
The Hidden face of Jesus by Margaret Magdalen 1994 DLT

66. Brian Thorne very carefully describes himself as a 'Christian who is a Counsellor'. He is best known as an expert on Carl Rogers and Person-centred Counselling. Christian books include "Behold the Man" (on the Passion of Jesus), "Divine Intimacy", and his local saint, Mother "Julian of Norwich".

67. A silence and a shouting – Meditations and prayers by Eddie Askew 1982
The cover of this Leprosy Mission Publication was the inspiration for the first Listening Post Logo.

68. I wish I had space to share with you the Easter 1998 edition of ACCord which describes the wonders of the "Continuing the Journey" Conferences a breadth of spirituality crossing denominational barriers.

69. Three steps forward, Two back by Charles Swindoll. Published by Bantam Books 1980. This book is about standing firm when faced with the deepest problem life offers; walking through setbacks for a better life tomorrow.
Charles Swindoll also wrote "Maybe its time to Laugh again and experience Outrageous Joy" Pub Word UK 1992,

70. Changes that heal by Dr. Henry Cloud, Pub. Zondervan Press 1992. He too quotes Philippians 2:12 "God is at work in our desires, and we need to bring them into relationship with Him (a thought central to John's dilemma and the answer to his every problem.)

71. "Love is a choice" by Roger Hemfelt, Frank Minirth, and Paul Meier, published by Zondervan Press is a book on co-dependency which offers hope especially in Part Five- "The ten stages of Recovery".

72. "Caring enough to confront" by David Augsburger
Published by Regal Books 1973.

73. Restoring the years of the locusts – Joel 2:25

74. "A Practical Workbook for the Depressed Christian" by Dr. John Lockley published by Word

75. "Forgiving the Impossible?" by Greta Randle. Inter-Varsity Press. 2010 by the current Chief Executive of ACC, Proof of God's healing power.

76. Fullness of Life. John 1:16

77. Immanence" is the quality in God which causes Him to be involved in the life of humanity and the world, and not stay remote from it. The chief evidence for God's immanence is the incarnation of the Son of God.

78. David Adam has written many books illustrating the "Celtic Way of Prayer", "the divine glory intertwined with the ordinariness of everyday events like the patterns on Celtic carvings and illuminated Gospels." Many of these have been published by Triangle Press including "The cry of the Deer", "Tides and seasons", and The Eye of the Eagle. (from 1985)

79. We based our thinking mainly around the book by Ian Bradley, "The Celtic Way, 1993, Darton, Longman and Todd, London, Ltd.
80. Joyce Huggett has been a great influence on my life, both from her many books of meditations such as "Open to God", "The smile of Love" and "Listening to God", "Listening to others" and "Finding Freedom". Hodder 1-6. These three are perhaps most directly relevant to the process of Christian Counselling Joyce and her husband Rev.David Huggetttwo led inspirational training events at ACC conferences

Part Four Counselling on the edge

81. The truth will set you free John 8:31 The nine "counselling on the edge" stories attest to it .
82. ACC Trauma and Abuse Group. www.tag-uk.net. Led by Mike Fisher.
83. Attachment. Trauma and Multiplicity. Working with Dissociative Identity Disorder. Ed Valerie Sinason. Routledge. London & Ny 2002 /2009.
84. The Void by Wendy Haslam, published by Author House 2009. Wendy is long term ACC SW representative colleague.
85. The addiction of a busy life by Edward England, Aviemore Books, GB 1998
86. Breathless by Gary Collins, published by Tyndale House, Wheaton, Illinois 1998
87. Care for the Family has become a major respected UK Christian Charity, campaigning and promoting initiatives in Christian Caring.
88. Oh God, Why? By Gerard W Hughes, published by Bible Reading Fellowship, UK 1993.
89. Strong in the broken places, Every Day with Jesus Nov/Dec 2005., written by Selwyn Hughes, Published by CWR UK
90. 2 Corinthians 12:9
91. To bind up the broken hearted, A Foundation in Christian Counselling by Mike Sheldon and Dave Ames, Foreword by Mervin Suffield – three of the Founders of ACC UK. Published by Mission to Marriage 1999.

Lightning Source UK Ltd.
Milton Keynes UK
UKOW041908120312

188836UK00001B/2/P